To all my fans ...

from Norm Who?

Norm Miller

Houston, Texas, USA

ISBN   978-0-9842746-0-4

Library of Congress Control Number: 2009938044

http://www.normwho.com

Printed in the United States of America.

Dedication

To my dad. He was such a fan of the game and just a great guy.

Table of Contents

Introduction

I am the answer to a baseball trivia question: Who scored the winning run in the Astros' longest, scoreless game?

On April 15, 1968, at 1:37 in the morning, I jumped on home plate in the bottom of the 24th inning to give us the victory, 1-0.

Every time I'm introduced as scoring that run, there is a ripple of excitement in the audience. It is time to set the record straight on just what a brilliant accomplishment that was.

I led off the 24th inning with a base hit, which made me 1-for-8. Now, that was a good night compared to many who went 0-for-10. After a couple of walks and an out, the stage was set for the Astros' favorite, Bob Aspromonte, to win the game. He stepped up to the plate with the bases loaded and one out. I took my lead off of third base, the pitcher wound up and delivered, and Bob hit a routine double-play ball to the Mets' Al Weis at shortstop. Al was so tired after being out there for six hours, he didn't get down quick enough and the ball went through his legs.

Here's where my talent really came through. I ran toward home plate and stepped on it.

I know what you're thinking: Big deal!

One of my fifteen minutes of fame

But a great story.

This book contains great stories, some humorous, some historic, and some personal, about my love affair with a great game.

Enjoy …

Norm Miller

Houston, Texas

http://www.normwho.com

Pay Cut, My Ass

Winter 1975. Even my father questioned what I was doing. His opinion was no better than that of the Atlanta Braves. They wanted to cut my salary - slash away with the big knife - and take away my hard-earned money.

"You're going to arbitration? Are you crazy or something? You should take what they give you and be quiet. Just be happy they are keeping you on the team."

That's my dad, a very conservative fellow. My mom - just the opposite - "Get all you can."

The way I looked at it, I've got rights. Everybody knows the Tom Seavers, the Bob Gibsons, and the Mickey Mantles of baseball. But what about the Norm Millers and the many like him?

Perhaps we're not the backbone of the game, but let's see them play without guys like us. I am living proof there is room for individuality in the game. Despite all of baseball's uniformity, I have lived by my wits.

I've roomed with Jim Bouton, the author of the first sports expose, *Ball Four*, lockered next to Hank Aaron and shared a hair dryer with Joe Pepitone. I've traveled in the same circles with all the characters of the game. But don't think it's been all that easy.

People took me for granted. For instance, I'm the guy who held the strobe lights for the photographers when they rushed in to snap pictures of Henry Aaron putting on his jock. I'm the guy that made sure if an ill-prepared reporter needed a sharp pencil, I had it. If a player ran out of cigarettes during the game, I would retrieve a pack from the locker room. This is important information that needs to get out.

Now this isn't to say that I haven't been around, seen the sights and heard the sounds. I was on the bench the night the Astrodome opened in 1965. I saw Willie Mays hit number 512 and break Mel Ott's National League home run record. I was on the bench when "Hammerin' Hank" hit number 715.

All this was on my mind as I flew to New York. It was the first year of arbitration and Norm "fucking" Miller was right in the middle of it.

Baseball had always had this system where you signed a contract to play, and they paid. When the year was over, they still owned you. You had no freedom to go anywhere else unless they traded or released you. In 1967 Curt Flood tried to fight the system in the courts and lost. How much leverage did players have? None. You would get an offer from the team, send it back un-signed, and repeat the process a couple of times. There were no multi-year contracts; there were no agents. The average salary back in '74 was $34,000. A big raise might be $10,000. I think Hank Aaron - after 700 plus home runs - was making $200,000.

Arbitration was brought in to try and speed up the process, so teams could get players to spring training. Like we had other choices.

My case was simple. I had been traded from the Astros to the Braves the previous year, bad back and all. In fact, when they called to welcome me, I told them not to make the deal. But they said they were told by the doctors I would be fine.

As it turned out, I wasn't fine and ended up playing in two games for the Braves, with eight at-bats. I did manage three hits and one dropped fly ball. I had two singles and a home run and drove in four runs. My salary was $35,000 and the bastards wanted to cut me $5,000 just because I spent 99% of the season on the disabled list. Of course, what went unnoticed here was, they traded a guy with a bad arm for one with a bad back, so who's to blame?

I marched into the arbitration room and took my seat across from Braves' General Manager, Eddie Robinson. I had known Eddie a long time; nice man but this was war.

I was being assisted by Dick Moss, assistant to Marvin Miller, the genius behind the players' union. Also Larry Fleischer from the NBA sat in. Firepower!

The arbitrator walked in wearing a seersucker suit and a bow tie. Goddamn, he looked like anything but a sports fan. Eddie Robinson opened up the proceedings.

"Good morning, Norm, how are you feeling?"

Oh, we're going to play the "good guy" role.

"Doing great; back's in great shape."

Eddie started off by saying that the Braves' position was a matter of principle. Bullshit, it's about $5,000. "I've known Norm for about 10 years. I've always felt he had never been given a fair opportunity to prove his talents."

True!

That I had always been regarded as a good hitter and a hard worker.

True again!

He pressed on, telling the arbitrator I was very popular with my teammates and then concluded by saying I was overpaid, but had been a very good negotiator throughout my career.

I leaned over to my counsel and whispered, "Is it too late to ask for a raise? This guy loves me."

Our case was simple. I was traded with a bad back. I even warned the Braves they might be getting damaged goods. I was traded for a sore-armed pitcher and there never had been a precedent for a player with a major injury being cut.

The arbitrator said he had heard enough. Handshakes were exchanged, and everyone proceeded to leave the room. Before I left, I took out a baseball card and autographed it for the arbitrator, hoping he had a son.

Three days later, a letter arrived. Justice had prevailed. My $35,000 salary was guaranteed for one more year.

Maybe this wasn't one of those landmark decisions you always read about. But it was a victory for the little guys. Now that it had been decided, it was time to get ready and head to spring training for the 12th time.

I was going to beautiful Palm Beach, Florida. That, in itself, was a relief. The previous ten years, spring training had been with the Astros in Cocoa, Florida. That's the place they hook up the hose to give the state an enema.

This was going to be an historic camp. Henry Aaron was approaching Babe Ruth's career home run record and the press came from everywhere and every planet. They flitted around like little green flies.

But a story they were missing was the one amongst the players. Four Braves had filed for arbitration. Two lost, one tied and then we had a winner: Me. Frank Tepedino had hit over .300 and lost in arbitration. Marty Perez, starting shortstop, lost. Darrell Evans hit 41 home runs and drove in everybody. He won, but I call it a draw because he didn't get the money he should have gotten. Norm Miller; eight at-bats, three hits, and a winner at arbitration.

The first day on the field, Ralph Garr and Dusty Baker just walked up to me and shook their heads. Then Darrell Evans came up and joined in. "How the hell can you win? You of all people!"

"What's wrong with all of you? I did my job. My god, most players with an injury like mine couldn't have gotten eight at-bats, let alone three hits. I rest my case."

My words didn't seem to console everyone. As Ralph Garr put it, "I have to play every day and get 200 hits to make $60,000. All you do is show up once in a while, take a massage and get $35,000."

Now, truth be known, I had been in the big leagues for a number of years. The average salary in '74 was $34,000, so I was just slightly ahead of the curve. As for the stars of the game, sure they were underpaid, but that was how the system took care of the owners. They owned you and they could threaten you, and what leverage did the players have? None. "Free agency" was still years in the future.

TV At 8

I was destined for success in baseball. At the age of eight years old, none other than Hall-of-Famer, Leo Durocher, predicted on national television, "Someday this boy will be playing in the major leagues," as he patted me on the head for the whole country to see. How ironic this would turn out to be when, many years later, Leo became my major-league manager.

The credit, however, goes to my dad, Irv Miller. At the age of one week, my father's first gift to his second son was not the typical stuffed animal. A large piece of leather was cast into my crib. I guess it was his way of saying that it sure would be nice to have a ballplayer in the family.

By the time I played my first Little League game, I could handle that leather pretty good. I grew up in Sherman Oaks, California, where the sun shines year-round and baseball was the thing to do. CBS television decided to highlight kids' baseball and brought their production crew to our Little League team. I was handpicked with a few, older kids to be on display nationwide on a Sunday afternoon.

It was a very exciting moment for our community that Sunday in 1954. All the parents got together and painted the ballpark, cut the grass, made sure the foul lines were straight. Setting a beautiful scene for the whole country to see.

Soon the stars of the show arrived. None other than Roy Rogers and Dale Evans. Even Trigger was there, and that made it good enough for me.

The special guest expert was Leo Durocher, a very big name in the game and just three years removed from the "miracle of Coogan's bluff." Bobby Thompson's shot heard around the world had brought down the National League pennant for the New York Giants.

Leo was managing the Giants against his former team, the Brooklyn Dodgers, and got his revenge against his nemesis, Branch Ricky, the Dodgers' General Manager and President, when Bobby Thompson hit a bases-loaded home run in the bottom of the ninth, which became baseball's "shot heard round the world."

Roy and Dale sang some songs, and Trigger performed his tricks, tearing up the field that everyone worked on so hard to get ready.

Then, it was show time. Leo grabbed a fungo bat, and the kids took the field. I was ready at third base. He put us through a fast-paced infield practice. It was one of those days when everything clicked for this eight-year-old. Leo called us into home plate. Roy, Dale and Trigger joined us. Leo put his hand on my head and said, "Folks, some day this kid will be in the big leagues." Trigger nodded.

Little League – The beginning

I grew up enjoying all the benefits Southern California had to offer; sun, girls, beaches and baseball all the time. We lived a block from the fields and my older brother, Mike, and I were really lucky to have a father that loved the game, and made it fun to practice and play. When he would get home from work, he was never too tired to go to the ballpark and hit ground balls, or pitch to us. "Get your glove down, throw overhand, get a good pitch to hit and hustle, hustle, hustle." The fundamentals of the game - he was so cool.

My Little League career was great. The harder I worked, the better I got. The only downside was all the attention I got turned me into a cocky brat.

There was no big-league baseball in Los Angeles in those days. My mom and dad would take my brother and me to Gilmore Field all the time to watch the Hollywood Stars, which were the Pirates' AAA team in the Pacific Coast League. Dick Stuart at first, Spook Jacobs at short and my favorite, the hot- headed Carlos Bernier, in center. I just couldn't get enough of the game. I watched how they hit, how they fielded - just amazed at how good they were. It was funny that they were doing all the things my dad kept telling me to do, especially the hustling part.

I Should Have Gone To Class

Then it was time to follow my brother into Van Nuys High School. He had played both baseball and football, and excelled in the classroom. Up to this point, I had showed little interest in the classroom. My reputation had preceded me, and I was ready to uphold it. My freshman year was not easy. First, my dad was diagnosed with tuberculosis, and was sent away to recover. My brother was off to college, so Mom had to deal with me. I wasted no time proving I was not like my brother. Class and I didn't get along. I got caught cutting school. I was called into the Vice Principal's office. Mr. Comerford called my mom in and announced he was going to discipline me. No sports for one year. I was going to be used as an example.

Let the rebellion begin.

Without my dad to hit ground balls; without my sports, what was left? Time for me to get even. The pranks are too numerous to mention, but let's just say the next year was hell for my mom.

I finally woke up and when my junior year came around, I was ready to go to class and get back on the fields. I was the starting quarterback for the junior varsity football team. I was small, maybe 5 foot 6, but I could throw. As I rolled out one play, I was tackled from behind, and when I hit the ground, I was piled onto. I felt a sharp pain in my lower back. When the bodies peeled off, I found I couldn't move. I was loaded into an ambulance and taken to the hospital. I was scared to death. It turned out not to be major, but it would take me some time to recover. I decided right there; no more football. Baseball was my future. So ended my gridiron career.

Our baseball coach at Van Nuys High knew nothing - zip - about baseball. Good guy, but useless as a coach. My junior year, I was the starting second baseman, and pitched. I did all right, but I think missing that one year, when I was being disciplined, either slowed me down or made everyone else better.

A Fireman Comes To The Rescue

The summer of my junior year, I tried out for a kind of a semi-pro traveling team. I was only 16, but, what the hell. The coach was a fireman named Jack Waldschmidt. That tryout turned out to be one of the most significant, defining moments of my life. My dad was still in the hospital, and my mom was just trying to keep me straight. My brother had gone off to college.

The team was going to play several games a week around the LA area, mainly against much older players. I was younger and smaller, but I had a good day. I hustled, I scuffled, caught everything hit to me, swung the bat with authority. The other players thought I was a pain in the ass because I kept jumping in front of them to get another ground ball, and begging to get back in the batting cage. I made the team.

Jack Waldschmidt was a blessing. He knew about my father and just never let me out of his sight. All summer he coached me, taught me about the game, and chewed me out when I had it coming, but most importantly kept my confidence sky high.

Back then, there was no draft as there is today. Teams would have tryout camps and hundreds would come. You usually had to be a high school senior or in college or over a certain age for them to look at you. Jack had a friend with the Los Angeles Angels (they were now a major-league team), and he convinced his friend to let me come to their four-day tryout camp.

I lasted the first three days, probably as a favor to Jack, but I did run well, field well and hit a lot of line drives. Anyway, on the last day, the players that hadn't been cut were going to play in a game so the scouts could see everybody under pressure.

Four hits later, I was the talk of the camp. As I was walking off the field at the end of the game, I was approached by an Angel's scout named Tufie Hashem. He put his arm around me and asked if my dad was with me. I told him about my dad and he asked if it would be possible to get his phone number and call him. I said, sure, and gave Dad's number to him. At that point, Jack walked up and talked with Tufie. We were joined by another scout, Bert Niehoff. The three of them chatted while I just swung my bat off to the side. I was 16; I didn't have a clue what's going on, but I did get four hits and was feeling really good.

We hopped in Jack's truck and headed for my home. He came in and told my mom that I had a great day and I might be getting some good news. Soon after Jack left, my dad called. He had been living in the City of Hope, in Duarte, California, a couple of hours from home. This had been devastating to our family, but the good news was that he was getting better and was soon to come home.

My mom handed me the phone. My dad, a very calm man, was very excited. The scouts had called him and asked if I could come down to Dodger Stadium when the team was in town (back then, the Angels shared the stadium with the Dodgers) and work out before the games. I couldn't believe what my dad was telling me. On the field? Before the games? Why me?

Dad's Home

There's no doubt in my mind to this day, that phone call to my dad was what finally healed him. Two weeks later, he was home and we were on our way to Dodger Stadium. We found the locker room and walked in. I had a locker waiting for me, number 54 hanging there. Bill Rigney, the manager, came over and introduced himself to my dad and me. He said he had heard a lot about me from Bert and Tufie, and to just have a good time out on the field. I looked around and there was Jim Fregosi, Albie Pearson - oh my god - Leon Wagner. Somebody pinch me.

An older fellow came up and introduced himself: "How you doing?"

"Great!"

"I'm Jack Paepke, one of the coaches. Now just get out there and be one of the guys. What position do you play?"

"Second base."

"Okay, good, you'll be working with Bobby Knopp. Great guy. We'll let you know when to come in to hit and everything else. Have fun." Jack spit some tobacco juice in a can next to my locker, gave me a wink and off he went.

I couldn't get dressed fast enough; even put my socks on backwards. The nerves had me shaking; my heart was pounding. Is this for real? I grabbed my glove and headed out to the field. I can't describe the feeling of entering a big-league dugout and looking out at Dodger Stadium. How many times had I looked into the dugout with binoculars from the bleachers, and now I'm coming out of it. I got a couple of pats on the ass from players, and coach Paepke came up and said, "Get out there son, let's see what you can do."

Shit, I'm 16 years old and I'm stepping out of a major-league dugout for the first time. I sprinted towards second base, watching Bobby Knopp take ground balls. He turned to me and asked my name.

"Norm Miller, sir."

"Well, Norm Miller, it's your turn. Hey son, don't look too good; I don't want to lose my job for a couple of years now."

I was paralyzed; my range was down to zero, my hands were made of stone, I must have booted the first five grounders. Relax, "stormin' Norman," you must be good or else you wouldn't be out here. Finally, the ball found my glove. Then another. How "bitchin" was this? We took grounders for about 20 minutes. Bobby suddenly headed towards the batting cage, looking back and telling me to come on, it's our turn. I forgot to bring my bat from the locker room, so I searched through the bat rack 'til I found one that didn't feel like a war club - something I could swing. I headed toward the cage. "You're in there next," Fregosi told me.

Shit, Jimmy Fregosi, all-star shortstop talking to me. Wow! Knopp took his last swing and headed towards first base. "All right, son, lay two bunts down, then hit and run and then 10 cuts."

The nerves weren't as bad; I laid down two perfect bunts, and then executed a perfect hit and run. I was in my world. I felt like every eye was on the kid in the batting cage. The pitches came in perfect speed, right down the middle, tailor made for my swing. Line drive, line drive, and, god, I was in heaven. "How many is that?" someone blurted out. I guess I was having so much fun, I forgot to count. Paepke yelled out, "This isn't the Norm Miller hour; one more and get out of there."

I unloaded and stood there watching one go deep. "Get the hell down to first, son, that ball doesn't have a chance of going out."

I sprinted to first; the ball didn't even reach the warning track.

For the rest of the summer, I worked out every home game the Angels had. I was the luckiest kid in the world.

16 years old and swinging with the pros

Sign On The Dotted Line

My senior year went well; lots of scouts were at all our games. I had a really good year, and when it came to an end, all I could think about was signing a pro contract. Colleges were calling, but, no way. I was going to sign and be a big-league ballplayer.

When it came down to signing, it turned out just two teams seemed really interested. The Angels, of course, and the Phillies. My small size and lack of power steered some teams away, and most decided my signing with the Angels was already a done deal.

The Phillies made an appointment and came over to our house to talk with my parents and me. They were really nice people. Paul Owens was the main man, and he said they wanted to take me up to Bakersfield where their Class A team played. They wanted me work out and get a feel for pro baseball.

Every big-league team has several minor-league teams – their "farm teams," where players who needed it got experience before being called up to the major leagues. You worked your way up from A ball, which has the least-proficient players, to AA and then to the top of the minor-league teams, AAA. Usually, a big-league team has a couple of A-league teams, one AA and one AAA team.

I thought, Bakersfield, hell, I had spent the summer working out with the Angels. But, I accepted and spent a weekend in Bakersfield. It was really fun hanging out with the young guys who were just starting their careers. I showed my skills and afterwards I was offered a contract. The signing bonus wasn't much - around $25,000 dollars total - but I was proud to get the offer.

We returned home and it was time to visit the Angels. By now, we knew Mr. Hemond, the farm director. Both scouts, Tufie Hashim and Bert Niehoff, were there. It was one of the most exciting moments of my life, and my parents were so proud. The money offer came and it was a little more than the Phillies offered. I wasn't going to be a big bonus baby, but I was going to be a professional baseball player - and for my home team. I signed. What a great day for our family!

Part of my signing bonus was a new car. It didn't take long to take delivery of a brand new 1964 Chevy "409" with four on the floor and chrome reverse rims. How cool was I?

Mom and Dad watch me sign my first contract with Bert Niehoff.

Signed, sealed and now it is time to deliver

Soon after signing, my picture was in the paper, "Local boy receives large bonus from Angels." Large was the word I used when they called. Perception is reality.

I had a couple of months to cruise around my home town, "the stud of Sherman Oaks."

Cruising To Spring Training

Then that day came when it was time to pack up the Chevy and head to my first spring training. I would be going right down the road about 40 miles to Anaheim, where all the Angels' minor league teams trained. I hugged Mom and Dad, backed out of the driveway and cruised down the freeway - my ass not even touching the seat. The only bad thing was that I couldn't see how cool I looked driving that car, but I knew everyone that saw me must have said, "There's that ballplayer, Miller, heading to spring training."

I approached the hotel, which was right across the street from Disneyland. Suddenly I hit the brakes. My god, the entire parking lot was full of 409s, 'vettes, Fords all jacked up in the front. It looked like a car show. I wasn't sure what to make of it. I threw it into gear and pulled right up and parked in the middle of all of them. Grabbed my suitcase and equipment bag and headed toward my room.

I put the key in the door and stepped in. It was dark, and then I heard a groaning noise and noticed a body rocking back and forth. Suddenly it rose. "Hey, roomie. Jim Sollami, outfielder."

"Norm Miller, second base."

"Where you from?"

"Sherman Oaks, right up the road."

"Great. I'm from Pennsylvania; flew all night, just getting some rest." He dropped back on the bed and started rocking back and forth again. I didn't know what the hell that was all about but - what the hell - he seemed okay. I unpacked and remembered I left something in my car. As I approached the lot, there must have been 15 guys around my car. "Is that yours?"

"Yeah."

"Solid lifters?"

"Nope."

"Cool rims."

"Thanks."

"Hey, pop the hood. That's nice." I was feeling pretty proud. Then I was challenged to a race. I quickly declined the offer; I didn't think it would be something the ball club would appreciate.

I went back to the room and I decided to wake Jim up and see if he wanted to eat. He said no, that he wanted to find out where a pool hall was and shoot some pool. He reached down and brought up a long box. He popped it open and pulled out a pool cue. "Look at this pearl inlay."

Hell, I didn't know what to say. "Shit that's cool, you must be good."

"Not too shabby! Grew up in my dad's pool hall, made a few bucks at it."

As I lay in bed that night, reality had set in. I was feeling a little homesick, scared, I mean I was on my own. I guess it was like my friends when they went off to college. I fell asleep and suddenly was awakened. "Eightball" Sollami had come home and was showing me a wad of money. "What a bunch of fish out there." He laid his cue down, and started that goddamn rocking back and forth. This is going to be something else.

So far, I'd been in spring training a couple of hours and met a pool hustler and a bunch of gear heads. Not one mention of hardball. That was all to change in a few hours.

I was awakened by the phone. "Hey, Eightball, get up, it's time for breakfast." We rolled out of bed, threw on our jeans and headed out the door. It looked like a pack of hungry wolves heading towards the lobby. We entered the banquet hall and it was already overflowing with ballplayers of all shapes, sizes and languages. This was so fucking exciting. The energy was sky high; the food consumption was amazing. Eightball and I joined a few others at a table.

"Hi, I'm Norm; this is Jim."

"Hey guys, where you all from?"

"Jim's from Pittsburgh: I'm from Sherman Oaks, right up the road." We sat down and ate like typical starving teenagers, talking with our mouths full. The egos were flying. Everybody fighting for a chance to recite their resume. "I was all city, hell, I was all state."

The bullshit was deep. Suddenly, we realized the room was almost empty and it was time to get to the ballpark.

We grabbed our equipment bags, threw them in my trunk and headed towards La Palma Park, right up the road. The parking lot was left with lots of skid marks. Kids will be kids.

When we entered the locker room, the procedure was kind of like being inducted into the Army. We signed paperwork, we got our uniforms and tried to find a locker. This was not the big leagues. Remember, I had already spent two summers working out with the big-league team, had my own locker, and a new uniform. But right now, it's three to a locker, retread uniforms and I'm loving it.

I couldn't get dressed fast enough; I couldn't wait to get on the field and show them what I could do.

Here we were, the future of the Los Angeles Angels. A couple hundred strong. Testosterone overflowing on the beautiful green grass of La Palma Park. All right, everybody at home plate. The dream was about to become a reality.

My God, I'm Not The Best!

Then, out of the dugout, here came the coaches. I looked for a familiar face, but these were all new. Most had wads of tobacco in their cheeks, spitting and looking at the group. Then, one stepped forward. "Gentlemen, I'm Al Monchak, I'm running this camp. And it's show or go time."

He had the look and presence of a drill sergeant. The next words to come out of his mouth were a total shock. "Where's Norm Miller?" Everybody started looking around, who is Norm Miller? Eightball jabbed me in the side, "Hey man, that's you." Shit, what the hell did I do? I choked and raised my hand. He stared at me and said, "Miller, you're mine." Not a good way to start.

"Outfielders to the outfield, infielders take your positions, pitchers and catchers to the bullpens, let's go." Guys were falling all over themselves. It was quite comical. I took my spot at second base, but those words, "You're mine," were ringing in my ears.

Within seconds, there were ground balls, fly balls, coaching, yelling, screaming, diving, leaping - it was fantastic. God, these guys could play. Out of the corner of my eye, I could see coach Al circling behind me. "You've got to charge that ball, Miller. Take another. Come on, you gotta have quick feet."

The workout was non-stop, the talent was endless and the coaching was great. I was called into the batting cage; it was time to show my stroke. I grabbed my bat, got into the cage and guess who took the mound? There was Al with a grin on his face. I don't know what happened; I just yelled out "Throw that shit over the plate." He glared, wound up and the battle was on. Line drive up the middle - Al ducked. He came up smiling and more determined. I just ripped everything he threw. I didn't notice it, but I was told later that nothing was going on during my time at the plate. The entire camp just watched this battle and wondered what it was all about.

"All right, everybody around the park, and Miller you better be first." I collapsed in my locker, too tired to take my shoes off. I just sat there for what seemed like hours. When I looked around, almost everyone was gone. I pulled my shoes off and then I was joined by the warden of the camp. He pulled up a stool. "Heard a lot about you, son. Proud of you, you set a great example today. You didn't let me down." Then he was gone.

As I lay in bed that night, cramping up, I was sure happy I didn't let the old bastard down.

Seven days a week, sunup to sundown, it was baseball at its best. I was so fortunate that I had a dad that taught me so well. There was no doubt it gave me a head start. As camp started its last week, the reality that I was in a business settled in. Rumors of where we were going to be sent to play were flying around, and then there was the talk of who might be going home. The dream would be ending for some of us.

I had my eyes on going to Hawaii, to play AAA for the Islanders. Hell, in my mind, I was 17 and ready. But as the days came down to a few, I started spending a lot of time with the group that coach Rocky Bridges was working with. Rocky was the manager of San Jose in the California league, Class A. Well, that's not too bad. It would be easy for my parents to come watch. The parking lot and clubhouse were thinning out. It was that time when dreams ended for some. Really sad.

Why Iowa?

It came down to the last night of spring training. I still didn't know for sure where I would be swinging the bat for money, and then the shocker. I was packing my bags and my dad was coming down to get my car to take home when I got the news. Davenport, Iowa, on a train the next morning. Iowa? You've got to be kidding. Class A, the Midwest League. I was sick, absolutely sick. Where was Iowa? I lay sleepless for hours.

We loaded up on the bus at 6:00 AM, 25 young ballplayers being shipped off to the wilderness. Three goddamn days on a train with a melting pot of personalities. After a change of trains in Chicago, we arrived in Davenport early in the morning. No one was there to greet us, but a massive rain storm. All we knew was, we had to find the Davenport Hotel. I always wished Norman Rockwell had been there to paint that scene. Twenty-five tired, lost souls, bats and bags in hand, soaking wet, looking up at the front of the Davenport Hotel in a rain storm. One expression on every face. This does not look good.

When my eyes opened the next morning and I looked around, I had forgotten where the hell I was. My god, the wallpaper, the carpet; how goddamn depressing. By the way, Eightball was still with me. We got up and went down the stairs to the lobby, or whatever it was. "You guys ballplayers?"

"Yeah."

"Wait out front; someone's on his way to get you." We went out front, the sun was shining. I looked around and boy, this was not LA. The rest of the guys slowly filed out. The troops were ready to be picked up.

Then we heard a screaming little man skipping up the street. "Hey guys, come on, follow me." Small, strange looking character, dressed in all white with a hunchback. What the fuck was this? "The ballpark's just a couple of blocks away." Off we went, but I swore to god, if this twerp turned down an alley, I was gone.

Then, there it was, Municipal Stadium, right on the banks of the Mississippi River. I entered the gates, and I have to say, I suddenly felt right at home. It was old, dark green and beautiful. We entered the clubhouse door, and standing right there in the middle of the room was Chuck Tanner, our manager. "Grab a locker, guys. Welcome to the Quad Cities." His enthusiasm was sky high. We threw our bags in the lockers and took a seat.

A silence overtook the room as our skipper walked in front of each locker, looking one-by-one into our eyes. "This is it, guys. For most of you, the start of a professional baseball career. I want to wish all of you the best of luck. The season opens in two days. You're all in great shape. I've seen you all for weeks in California, and I know we are going to be one hell of a team. So let's get unpacked and on the field."

Chuck Tanner, former major leaguer with the look and enthusiasm of a Marine. I couldn't wait to walk through the tunnel and play for the "Chuckster."

I stepped onto the field and just looked out toward center. Well, this was beautiful. It reminded me so much of Gilmore Field, where I had watched the Hollywood Stars for years.

We worked out; ground balls, fly balls, line drives. You can't imagine the feeling of being a professional ballplayer, no matter where it is.

None of us young guys had a real clue about what life was going to be. I knew I didn't want to stay in the hotel long, so somewhere to live was top priority. My salary was $500 a month for about five months. Jack Haines, a second-year pitcher, had his car waiting for him when we arrived - a veteran move. He offered to drive a few of us around to look for housing. The bottom floor of a two-story house, with one large room, a kitchen and a bathroom, was the best we could find in two days. It would sleep five and the landlord, an old, old woman, would also do our laundry. All this for $10 a week, per player. Need I say any more? What a deal! Five guys, one room, "Camp Davenport." Welcome to the minor leagues.

We departed the Davenport Hotel and moved in. Under closer examination, we realized that not all sleeping arrangements were equal; so a coin toss decided who got the bed with lumps, who got the couch with lumps and stains, who got the mattress on the floor, and the bunk beds were the bonus for the two winners. I got the couch.

The bathroom was quaint. Located directly off our living area, it had two basic features: no soundproofing, and a toilet that you had to sit side-saddle on to make it all work. I couldn't wait to see how the laundry deal worked out.

Opening Day

We were one day away from opening day, but first there was the parade. Saturday morning we were loaded into convertibles and paraded around the Quad City area, as it is known. Davenport, Moline, Bettendorf, and just across the muddy Mississippi was Rock Island, Illinois. We waved to the fans; this was really a hoot. I must say, though, the quality of attractive women was not up there on the scale of California. Saddle shoes with socks was not quite what I was used to. Anyway, I was there to play baseball. Now concentrate, it's opening day.

The stands were filled and the music was loud when I stepped out of the home dugout for my first professional game. I just stood there looking out, taking it all in. I'm not sure how many people Municipal Stadium held, but it looked filled, just like I had seen Dodger stadium so many times.

They were still doing last-minute details to the stadium. In center field, a man on a ladder was putting the finishing touches on a brightly painted sign. "Hit it over this sign and win a …"

Chuck called us all together down the left field line. We surrounded our leader and his words were like magic. He started slowly and ramped up into hysteria. "This is it guys. Opening day comes once a year. This is your chance; this is your dream. Remember the fundamentals, believe in what got you here and just remember, you can't win them all if you don't win the first. Go get 'em!"

Burlington, Iowa, was our opponent. I took the field at second. There was Art Miranda, my double play partner, at short. Bob Hiegert, a fellow Californian, at third. Bob Johnson at first, Jim Tokas out in right and my buddy, Eightball, in left. Edmundo Borrome in center and the cagey veteran, Pete Gongola, behind the plate. On the mound, the crafty right hander, Mike Carubia.

This was fucking great. The mayor came out and bounced the first pitch up to the plate; the fans booed. Carubia threw his last warm-up pitch, Gongola threw the ball down to second and around the horn it went.

PLAY BALL! The 1964 Midwest League season - and my quest for fame and fortune - had begun.

After three up and three down, we rushed into the dugout. I was hitting third, of course. I went to the bat rack, grabbed my helmet and bat and stood on the steps of the dugout, taking it all in. The butterflies were indescribable. Two quick outs and I approached home plate. The crowd was roaring. I happened to glance out towards center field and noticed, "Hit the ball over the fence and win a free steak at Cattleman's." I swung from my ass and struck out.

We lost 2-0; I went 0-for-4. That goddamn sign. The fans poured out of the stadium, disappointed I'm sure. But as Chuck told us after the game, "The great thing, guys, is we get to do it all over again tomorrow."

I lay on that couch all night. Tomorrow couldn't come fast enough for me. I couldn't stop thinking about 0-for-4. All those fans, I'm never going to make it to the big leagues doing that. Hell, I won't get out of Iowa.

Ass Kicked

It was Sunday, the fans were back and I was keyed up. I'll show them. The first time up, I popped up for the third out. I didn't hustle to first base, and when Art brought my glove out, I grabbed it and flung it to the ground.

It got worse. I booted the first ground ball hit to me. A routine play and my hands turned to stone. Now I'm in a rage, kicking dirt, going nuts. Gongola steps out in front of the plate and yells, "Come on, asshole, get over it."

The error caused no harm; the inning ended and I headed toward the dugout. Suddenly, I was yanked by my shirt from behind and dragged into the locker room. It was our skipper. He spun me around and lifted me off the ground and slammed me against the locker. He was fuming. Veins popping up in his neck, his eyes looking right through me, foaming at the mouth. I have never been so scared in my life. "Listen, you son of a bitch. This is a man's game and what you did out there will never happen again. It's not about you, you hear me? I don't give a fuck where you came from or what you did in high school, that behavior was bush league. You are going to be a professional. You hear me?" I couldn't answer because I was choking and scared shitless. He went on and on and then just dropped me.

That night after the game, I was so fucking disappointed in myself, I seriously contemplated jumping off the bridge into the Mississippi. A couple of the guys came by my locker. "Come on, let's go get a pizza, you'll be all right." I decided that would probably be a better idea. The Village Inn was just a block away. I was too young for a beer, but I wasn't too young to get some advice from a cagey veteran, Pete Gongola. "One horseshit game and you're already nuts. In about a week, you'll be in a straight jacket."

We had two more games at home before our first road trip. I decided to lower my expectations of going for the fences. I got my pitch and ripped it up the middle. As I stood at first, I looked over to the skipper for a sign. A couple of claps and even a little smile went a long way. I got the steal sign on the second pitch and I was gone. Safe! Now this is more like it. Artie and I turned our first double play that game, and how quickly things can change. Boy, the pizza sure tasted better after that game. We finished our first home stand with two wins and I managed a couple more hits. It was time to hit the road.

Road Trip!

It was 8:00 AM, and we were outside the stadium, sitting on the curb; equipment piled up, waiting on the bus. We were opening that night somewhere in Wisconsin, wherever that is.

Chuck Tanner was pacing. Then, bouncing across the parking lot, came the Quad City Angel Express. It came to a screeching halt. The door flew open and the bus driver stepped out. About 30, peculiar, with a very large nose. "Had to pass my driving test."

"Did you?" Chuck asked.

"I'm here, aren't I?" We threw the bags on the bus and loaded up. Gongola asked the driver his name. "Pecker." With a roar of laughter, we were off.

The bus gave all the appearance of making at least its third comeback. A seven-hour excursion awaited us; destination, Wisconsin Rapids.

After our three-game series in Wisconsin Rapids, a quaint Midwest town, we were off to Appleton, Wisconsin. As I stared out the window looking at the waves and waves of corn, I noticed how dark it was getting on the horizon. Just like a curtain of night was closing in on us. Then I saw a funnel reaching down toward the ground. I walked up front to the Pecker and asked him if that could be a tornado. He glanced to the right and said, "Sure is, we get them all the time up here."

Pecker was right. Tornadoes, monsoons, hail - the heartland of America had it all.

The season continued, winning some, losing some and a hell of a lot of games called for weather. We even had a game called because the fish flies, as they were called, were so thick one night, we couldn't see a thing.

The travel was seldom easy. Bumpy roads, a bus that was not built for comfort or speed and, I swear to god, everything looked the same. Besides Wisconsin, we visited the wonderful Iowa metropolises of Clinton, Cedar Rapids, Burlington and my all-time favorite, Dubuque. Now, Class A is the low minor leagues, where the motivation is to do well and move up. Well, Dubuque accelerates your will. Our hotel had an elevator for two at a time, depending on your size. This was not an Otis. My room was on the fourth floor. As I walked in, I noticed a large rope on a hook next to the window. "Hey roomie what's the rope for?"

"Hanging yourself after a bad game." I approached the window, opened it and looked down. Then it came to me. In case of fire, throw the rope out the window. I tested the theory. It worked, except you came to your rope's end at the second floor. From there, it was, let go and pray.

Dubuque was also home of John Petrakis Stadium. Up to now, the ballparks had been pretty nice. Old, green ballparks; just what you would expect in the 60's Midwest. Well, this was the all-timer. First, let me describe the playing field. Rocks in the infield, rocks in the outfield. All sizes, shapes and colors. We were, in fact, told that it was originally a rock garden. Now, that's a fucking shocker.

The final thing about Petrakis Stadium was the cinder-block locker room. Approximately a 20 x 20 building with a door. Inside it was simple: nails driven into the cinder blocks for hanging your clothes, a hose for washing off and a drain. And who could ever forget the bundle of rags that we could use to dry off with - old boxer shorts with buttons still in place, sweaters; you can just imagine. We dressed and showered at the hotel the next two nights.

Ouch!

Soon, the days turned into weeks and weeks into months. I was doing what was expected of me. Approaching the halfway point in the season, I was among the leaders in several categories, including eating free steaks courtesy of Cattleman's. The team was playing well. Hard not to play all-out for a guy like Chuck Tanner. I really think that's why I ended up in Davenport and not in San Jose my first year. Rocky Bridges was not the toughest to play for. The scouting report on me probably was, "needs some maturing." Tanner was the right guy for me.

I was having one problem in the Midwest. I was not getting laid. I had a couple of things working against me. No car and four roommates. It was hard enough to get a girl to go home with you, but to sell them the story that, "It's okay, they're all asleep;" - they weren't buying. Here I was, a young, pretty good-looking professional baseball player from southern California, and at this point I would settle for just getting my hand on one tit. Just one tit. Whenever I had a bad game, I knew it was "sperm backup."

As we approached the half-way point of the season, we had a visitor, Tufie Hashem, one of the original scouts that had signed me. There were rumors floating around that I might move up and out of the Midwest League. I was praying to go anywhere. Tufie followed the team for about a week; we talked, but no hints on what was happening.

Then bad luck came. I hit a ground ball up the middle and as I lunged for first base, I collided with the first baseman and went head over heals. At first, I felt fine, but a few minutes later when I got a ground ball at second, I suddenly couldn't raise my arm to throw it. The pain was excruciating. The hunchback trainer came out to see what was wrong. He advised the skipper I should come out of the game, and be sent to the hospital for x-rays.

The diagnosis was a mild separation. I was out for a couple of weeks. They hung my arm in a sling and sent me back to my couch. When I entered our swankienda, a party was going on. I played the sympathy role as much I could, and, thank god, one of those darling Midwest delights fell for it. It wasn't easy in a three-point stance, but I had to do it.

Sent Home To Hide

A round 2:00 AM, everybody was gone and I was sleeping quite well, even with the shoulder pain, when the phone rang. It was Tufie and he wanted me to grab a cab and come downtown to the Blackhawk Hotel where he was staying.

In a matter of minutes, I entered his room. "What's your dad's home phone number?" I gave it to him. "Irv, it's Tufie. I know it's late but I wanted to let you know Norm will be flying home tomorrow." He went on to tell my dad about the injury and instructed him to pick me up and go visit Roland Hemond, the farm director at the Angels' office. That was it. So I went back to pack, woke up the guys and told them good-bye, and off to the airport.

I was in a lot of pain when I landed at LAX. It was great to see my dad. I assured him the injury wasn't serious, and we sped off to our meeting. I was thinking they were going to let me rest at home for a couple of weeks and then off to Hawaii, AAA.

Little did I know when I entered Mr. Hemond's office, my life was about to change. Mr. Hemond explained a draft rule that was going to prevent them from being able to protect me on the major-league roster. So they had come up with this plan to announce I was going to have surgery; my career was in question, and the point of this exercise was to make other teams forget me.

So, to the beach I went, really missing playing and the guys. It took a few weeks for my shoulder to heal and then the ball club started working me out at a ballpark in Hollywood, where nobody would see me. Ground balls, batting practice, just me and a couple of scouts. I also went to a lot of games at Dodger stadium, my arm in a sling. The message to anyone who asked was I had surgery, pins were placed in my shoulder and it didn't look good for my future.

I was being paid to lie - on the beach.

As the winter draft approached, I started getting calls from scouts about my shoulder. "Oh, it's bad, still in a sling." Most of them were buying the bullshit, I thought.

One scout, a man named Al Hollingsworth, called more than others. The night before the draft, he called once again. "Son, I was in Davenport the night you got hurt. I also called the hospital that night and, well, let's say they didn't cover up the truth very well. We have the first pick tomorrow and how do you feel about becoming a Colt 45?"

I asked what league they played in, because to be honest, I knew nothing about them. "National League and we sure think a lot of you." All those summer days on the beach, all the secret workouts and all that acting and I was about to become a Colt 45.

The Plan Backfired

The next morning as I was driving to the beach, I heard the announcement on the radio. "Local prospect, Norm Miller, was drafted by the Colt 45's." I'd be lying if I said I was happy. Texas, shit.

Here I was, 18 years old and going through a major change of life. From an Angel to a Colt 45, whatever the hell that is. I thought it was a malt liquor.

Time was on my side. I had a couple of months to do some homework. Burning questions kept infiltrating my mind. Like, where is Houston? Who was on the team? I grabbed the Atlas and a stack of baseball cards. I was never good in geography and really didn't realize just how big Texas was. There it was. A good ten inches from Los Angeles. I visualized a city of horses and cowboys, and that was okay. I loved John Wayne movies. As I perused my card collection, I started pulling out all the Colt 45's. Norm Larker, Jim Owens, Turk Farrell, Bob Aspromonte, Felix Mantilla, Rusty Staub. What the hell is a "Rusty Staub?" Houston was an expansion franchise, and being a homey, I really only cared about the Dodgers and Angels, up to this point in my life.

I received a letter from the front office. They notified me that I would be starting camp with the big boys, and my salary was going to take a significant jump to $650 a month. Well, everything is bigger in Texas. Good start.

Heading To The Swamp

The time came closer to head for my second spring training. This time, I would be training in Cocoa, Florida. After a long cross-country flight and an hour's van ride, we pulled up to the Astros' spring training base. This was the year that everything was going from cowboys to spacemen. The Astrodome was opening, and the team had a new name. It was around midnight and all I could see was this large brick square building painted turquoise blue. I grabbed my bags with great anticipation and walked into the lobby. It had the look of a hotel, but then again, it didn't. It was quiet as a monastery.

I checked in at the front desk, and was given a key. Up the stairs, I dragged my bags, down the hall and still no sounds or movement. I opened the door. It was dark; I stood there 'til my eyes adjusted a little. I could see there were two single beds, and it looked like a big lump was in the far one. I moved closer and at the top of this lump was a bald head on the edge of the pillow. A coach; shit, I'm rooming with a coach. I pulled out my portable record player and threw on some Beatles. The lump leaped. "Turn that shit off, you looney tune." He rolled over and went back under the covers. Probably didn't like the Beatles. Probably Montovani would have been a better selection.

As the sun came up, you could hear in the distance a banging on doors and screeching. "Wake up, you didn't come here to sleep; it's time for some hardball." I jumped up and my roomie came out of the bathroom. There he was, maybe five-foot-eight, stocky and still old looking.

"Sorry about last night, coach."

"Coach, my ass. Get out of my way." I took a quick shower to wake up and when I came out, I was greeted with a smile. "Hey kid, Bill Heath, catcher!"

"Norm Miller, idiot." He claimed to be 30, which would have made me 14. I threw on my jeans and followed Bill out the door, down to the back of the fortress and into a cafeteria. Here we go again, the first day. Lots of good food. Lots of energy.

I recognized a few of the faces around the room from my card collection. Bill explained that he also had been drafted from the White Sox organization and that this was his first year with the Astros.

We finished eating, went upstairs to get our equipment and head over to the "big-league" clubhouse. On our way, we noticed there were four fields, a stadium, a lake and we were surrounded by swamp. Then I saw the first of many signs posted around the complex. "Snakes, watch where you walk." I didn't like that.

As we walked into the clubhouse, I was surprised how small it was. An old man was standing just inside the door. "What are your names?"

"I'm Heath; that's Miller."

"Heath, you're down there. Kid, you're back by the "shitter." I quietly walked past Aspromonte, Mantilla and two mean-looking guys, who stared right through me.

I found my locker as far back as one could be. Number 76 was hanging there. I unpacked and just looked around. I was starting over. Nobody here knew me; I had to get noticed and make the most of whatever time I had here with the big guys.

Before taking the field the first day, our manager, Luman Harris, gave a little talk. If this guy wasn't the "spitting image" of John Wayne, I don't know who was. I love John Wayne; what a coincidence, I thought. Just a few southern words and out we went. I wanted to be first out the door, but given my locker's geographical location, last would have to do. There I was, walking onto the field with "major leaguers." Guys that had played for years. Sure, I had worked out with big leaguers, but this was different. These guys were my teammates, if only for a short time before I went to my next minor-league team.

I was surprised at the countless hours we spent on fundamentals. Pitchers covering first base on a ball hit to the right side of the infield. Outfielders hitting the cut-off men with their throws. Taking countless ground balls, pop-ups; you name it, we worked on it. I learned this stuff when I was in Little League from my dad, yet it was the same stuff being worked on by big leaguers. What does that tell you about the game?

Time To Get Noticed

I felt like I was doing good, but not standing out. Paranoia? One day after taking our final lap around the field, it was time to stop being the quiet rookie and have some balls and speak up. As we made our final lap around the field and everyone headed in, I approached one of the coaches and asked for more work. "I'm not tired; I need some more ground balls." And then I asked for some help with my bunting, knowing that would get me in one of the cages. As dark came, I flipped on the lights and worked on my hitting. The coach said it was dinner time, why don't we take it in? Not hungry. "Then turn out the lights when you are." He smiled and headed in.

By the time I got in the clubhouse, the laundry was being done and they were sweeping up. I was starved, but what the hell, maybe that night would pay off some day.

A couple of more days of the same plan, and something interesting happened. There were a few other rookies in camp, but they were asked to pack up and join the minor-league camp. I was told I would be sticking around for a few more days. Well, in a few more days, the Grapefruit League was beginning

The Grapefruit League was games between teams who held spring training in Florida. We would travel around Florida playing practice games. In Arizona, they did the same thing, but it was called the Cactus League.

That day came and the Astros would be playing the Minnesota Twins. Wow! As the Twins' bus pulled up that morning, there was Tony Oliva, Rod Carew, Harmon "fuckin" Killebrew carrying their bags to the visitors' clubhouse. I felt like I was on sacred ground as they walked by me.

Sitting on the bench, taking it all in, I was just beside myself. So much so that I didn't hear my name called from the other end of the bench. "Hey kid, the skipper wants you; get your ass down there." Luman Harris, the manager, told me to get a bat and lead off the bottom of the inning.

"Are you "shitting me?" I scrambled through the bat rack, looking for my bat. Grabbed a helmet and stumbled out of the dugout. Grapefruit games don't mean much to most, but to me, well, this may be as close as I ever get. On the third pitch, I swung late, but ripped a line drive to the left center field gap. I rounded first and as I hit second, I let out a "yahoo." I headed towards third, I dove head-first into the bag; "safe." I got up, the fans were cheering. Jim Busby, the third base coach, came over, patted me on the ass and whispered, "Easy on that yahoo shit." It's a good thing the game ended with the next batter. If I had gotten up again, there is no doubt the pitcher would have drilled me for showing him up.

I have always thought that those few extra nights I stayed out by myself did get me noticed. I believe that's why I got an extra day in the big camp and the opportunity to hit a triple. The next day I was sent down.

Going Down Was Inevitable

As I walked into the minor-league clubhouse, the only thing I cared about was the location of my locker. The clubhouse boy showed me the way. What a breath of fresh air.

Since the Astros were one of the few teams which had their minor league and major-league training in the same place, being sent down to the minors meant walking to a different clubhouse and playing on a different field in the same complex.

The Astros' complex had four fields, and they used them all. This gave everyone the opportunity to get a lot of work. It was non-stop, other than a short break for lunch. If you were not catching ground balls or running the bases, you were in the batting cages, swinging away or bunting. Lots of chatter, lots of enthusiasm. It also gave us the chance to watch major-league games close up. Another advantage was that while you were over on the minor complex you could just look over the fence and see where you wanted to go. Very motivating.

At night, it was great food and all you had left was enough energy to go to bed. The minor leaguers were four to a room, eight to a bathroom. I was still with Bill Heath, and that was really nice. After a couple of weeks of hard work, I really needed to get out of that joint. Curfew was midnight. The camp was located about 20 miles west of Cocoa Beach. I hitched a ride down to the beach with a couple of the other guys. The place I had heard about was the Vanguard Lounge. This was where it was happening. I was only 18, but maybe I could sneak my way in for a peek. So I was sitting at the bar, enjoying a beer, trying to be cool. Two meat hooks suddenly grabbed me and threw me out the door into the sand. As I rolled over - kind of shook-up because it happened so damn fast - there were two familiar faces: Turk Farrell and Jim Owens. Large, mean-looking men. When I was in the big-league clubhouse the first couple of weeks, these two guys kind of commanded a lot of respect. Their joint nickname was the Dalton Gang. "Don't you ever come into any major-league bar where we are again, you bush-league punk."

A lesson was learned, and for the remaining nights, the Vanguard was not on my agenda.

We started playing intra-squad games in the about the fourth week of camp. These games would last forever. Sometimes you would come out of the lineup, and three hours later back in. There was a central tower, where the powers-that-be could watch all four fields at once. In a short period of time, players had to be evaluated and determined where, or if, they were going to play baseball for a living.

Meanwhile, the major-league team was getting ready to wrap up the Grapefruit League and head to Houston for the opening game of the Astrodome against the New York Yankees.

I was playing second base working on double plays. I got knocked on my ass trying to turn a double play. Time out was called. Then I noticed the gates opening down the third base line, and a golf cart racing my way. It came to a sliding stop at second. I yelled "safe." Some laughed, but the driver didn't appreciate it. I got up and brushed off my uniform, as this tall, kind of odd-looking man exited the golf cart.

"Son, give me that glove. You're going to get your ass put right out of baseball, if you don't get rid of the goddamn ball quicker. You've got to hit that bag and get the hell out of the way," as he demonstrated. "Goddamn rookies." He climbed back in his cart and was gone like the Lone Ranger.

"Who the hell was that?"

Coach Churn smiled, "My boy, that was the boss, Paul Richards, the general manager."

The next morning at breakfast, Luman Harris came over to my table and told me to report to the big-league clubhouse for the game that day. It was to be the last game. "Oh, and by the way pack your bags; you're going to Houston with us tonight."

I ran upstairs and started throwing all my shit into my suitcase. I had no idea what that was all about. I headed over to the stadium and back to my shit-house locker. As I was putting on my uniform, The Turk got in my face. "Hey, kid, don't fuck up today; I'm pitching."

As I grabbed my glove to head out for batting practice, Coach Busby stopped me at the door. "Hey, son, you're leading off and playing second. Joe's getting a rest today." Joe being Joe Morgan, a rookie sensation in the making.

"I'm what?"

"Starting! Think you can deal with that? We can get someone else."

"No, that's great." I headed back to the shitter to throw up.

I overcame my initial fear, anxiety and everything that comes with your first start. I had a good game, got a couple of hits and didn't boot any balls, so take that, Turk.

The Things Rookies Have To Do

The buses were loading up to head to the airport in Orlando. I was finishing packing my bags at my locker when I suddenly noticed two large feet. Guess who? Turk handed me a cardboard box. "Have this in my locker tomorrow night and don't fucking open it or let it out of your sight." He turned and left. The box had holes in the top. It also had something alive in it. The life of a rookie.

I boarded the bus last, box in hand, and retreated to the back of the bus. I don't like creatures from swampy areas, and I could only imagine what I was in charge of.

It had been a long camp, and now we're off to Houston. Upon landing, we loaded up charter buses and were taken to downtown Houston to a nice hotel. I finally got a chance to call my folks and tell them I was in Houston with the team.

The opening of the Astrodome in '65 was a worldwide event. The first indoor stadium, being billed as the "eighth wonder of the world." Judge Roy Hofheinz, one of the owners of the Astros, had conceived the concept and got it built. We had heard so much about it in camp; and everywhere you turned were pictures of the structure, but we were not prepared for what we were going to see later that day.

Up to that point in my life, just walking into any stadium was a thrill. The sight of the green grass, the painted signs on the fences; it just worked for me. Ballparks were all shrines. I just love this game.

The buses rolled down Main Street on our way for the first workout at the Houston Astrodome, home of the newly-named Astros. Everyone was looking out the windows in great anticipation. The further we went down Main, the worse the neighborhood looked. We turned left, past a small amusement park and a few seedy motels. Then all of a sudden, there it was.

This can't be a ballpark. It looked like it had just landed from outer space. We cautiously approached the unknown. Through the double doors, down the stairs. Entering something for the first time is very intimidating. We were lead to the concourse, and suddenly there we were. Jaws dropped, eyes bulged - our first encounter with the unknown. Enormous! Imagine indoor baseball. Yes, it had an infield, and fences way out there. But, my god, a roof? Nobody was moving or saying anything definitive. Just oohs and aahs. Frozen in our disbelief; this was the new home of baseball and it belonged to the Houston Astros.

The next stop was the clubhouse. There was no let-down as we entered. The size was immense. The lockers were small rooms. The training room, my god, was a small hospital. This truly made a fellow proud to be an Astro.

I looked for my locker; there it was, Miller. I only wished I had enough stuff to fill it. There was such a state of shock amongst the players, nobody was moving. I was just sitting there with my cardboard box in my lap. "All right, guys, let's get unpacked, downstairs and get loose."

I looked around, taking in the moment, and here came Turk. He grabbed the box from my lap and walked away, saying nothing. You're welcome, asshole, I thought to myself. The pace turned frantic, as everybody wanted to get down on the field of play for the first time. Down the stairs, under the seats and up some stairs, and suddenly you were in the longest dugout in the history of mankind. Later, I was to learn that Judge Hofheinz, the owner, was told that people always want seats over the dugout and are willing to pay for the privilege. So the Judge made the dugouts as long as he could.

The press had come from all over the world, and they were filming every nook and cranny of the building. From ground level, looking up to the top of the ceiling was like looking into space. Of course, what was on everyone's mind was, can a batted ball hit the ceiling? It was so high, it seemed impossible.

Between players, coaches, management and media, the place was packed. A regular workout was underway. But it didn't take long for some bad news. First of all, the grass infield was terrible. The grass was more like hay. Second of all, fly balls to the outfielders were not being caught because you couldn't see them. The trouble was the Plexiglas roof. Not enough sunlight was getting in to grow the grass, and too much glare was blinding the outfielders. This was worldwide news. The media took no time jumping on all this. The Astrodome in '65 cost $32 million and within hours was being hailed as a "colossal flop."

For the next few days, workouts continued, but oh, those problems with grass and glass. People with all kinds of ideas from the sublime to the ridiculous started to appear. Especially what to do about the fly ball situation. I was sent out as the guinea pig with a helmet on as different colored balls were hit in the air. Balls that beeped and everything imaginable. But no solution. Then the engineers decided about all they could do with opening day just about upon us was to paint the Plexiglas roof black. It worked, we could see the fly balls, but the paint also caused another problem. Less light getting in caused the grass to deteriorate even more. So, as opening day approached, the grass infield was thinning out rapidly and green paint was being applied to the dirt being exposed. The fly ball situation improved, so the regular outfielders slowly started to creep out into their positions, giving me a much-needed rest.

The day before the opening exhibition game against the Yankees, I was called into Luman Harris's office and told I would be there for the first of three games and then I was off to AA at Amarillo.

With the entire town - in fact, the state - ready to roll out the Astrodome and final touches being put in place, I entered the locker room for my last appearance before I headed back to the minors. I walked into the locker room and there it was, the answer to the burning question: What was in the box I carried all the way from Florida? Turk was walking his baby alligators on leashes around the clubhouse. And this was just the beginning of a very interesting and monumental evening.

The stands were filled early, the anticipation obviously at a fever pitch. The new-look Astros were about to unveiled. I sat in my locker, putting on my game uniform when Juan Quintana suddenly screamed and literally climbed up in his locker. I jerked around and, oh my god, a snake. I mean a mother fucking large snake was sliding across the floor heading right for us. I bolted, almost killing myself tripping over chairs. Players were heading out the door. Total chaos in the clubhouse. In all his splendor, Turk in the middle of the locker room was laughing his ass off. George, as he called it, was his pet boa constrictor, and George crawled right into my locker. Now, we're talking about eight feet of snake. Thank god Mike White, an outfielder, was not afraid. He approached the snake, grabbed it and pulled it out of my locker. But George decided to spray shit all over my uniform, which I had dropped on the floor. So I was a little late for the opening ceremonies. "Get me through this night and off to Amarillo, where I belong."

The rest of the evening was sensational. The opening was spectacular, the first ever exploding scoreboard was a smash, and the world loved the Astrodome. I didn't get in the game, but who cares? Just to be there was an honor and a horror. Seeing Mickey Mantle hit the stadium's first home run ever was awesome, and seeing "George the boa" shit in my locker was not.

Off To The Panhandle

The next morning it was Trans Texas Airways. Twin-engine, prop plane headed to the Panhandle of Texas. I looked out the window, thinking about all I had been through the past few weeks. It was almost a relief to get it over with and have time to think about my second year of playing pro baseball. AA, the Texas League, being a step up. I just wondered what it was going to be like.

You can fly all day and still be in Texas. Finally we started going down; as I gazed out, I saw nothing. We were going down, but into what I didn't know. Amarillo, Texas, in all its splendor. Right in the middle of nowhere and brown. Just dirt brown.

I was met by Ward Goodrich, the GM of the Amarillo Sonics. On the ride to the hotel, Mr. Goodrich said the town was looking forward to the young California kid coming to play. I was pretty clueless that as you moved up the ladder, the towns got a little bigger and took their minor-league teams a little more seriously. That means they actually had a reporter in Cocoa for a while, and they were making a big deal of me coming to Amarillo.

I was dropped off at the Downtowner Motel, where I saw most of my teammates. They had been there a couple of days working out while I was in Houston. I checked in and it was time to head out with the guys to Potter County Stadium, the home of the Sonics. This was the first year the Astros had this affiliation in Amarillo. The team was previously the Gold Sox, but in keeping with the new "space" theme, they had become the Sonics.

Twenty hours earlier, I'd been in the "eighth wonder of the world," and now I was pulling up to Potter County Stadium, located at the fairgrounds. AA is a step up from where I had been last year, but Potter County Stadium was a nosedive down. I got out of the cab and walked out to the field. What a beauty. I was speechless. This country-bumpkin ballpark had not changed in years. I walked out to second base and it was hard and dusty. The stands were faded green, and it smelled.

I headed into the clubhouse, which was about as small as it could be and still be somewhat functional. Freshly painted; I could only imagine how many coats of paint had preceded the one they just put on. Proof of its days as a Yankees franchise, carved in wood in my locker was "Joe Pepitone was here." That's the beauty of the minor leagues, someone you idolize or watched on TV has always been where you're trying to go.

A new year, new teammates, a new manager, but the same goals. Swing hard in case I hit it, run like hell and have some fun.

Speaking of managers, Lou Fitzgerald from Knoxville, Tennessee, was the man. Quite a contrast to Chuck Tanner. I had been around Lou a little in spring training; he didn't seem to say much, and so far he just sat in his office smoking a cigar. He stopped by my locker and wanted to know how things went in Houston. I started to tell him, but he lost interest pretty quickly. Blew some smoke in my face and out the door.

A few of the guys I didn't know came over to introduce themselves. Unlike Davenport, which was mostly young guys, this team had a strange mix of older guys, a couple of young guys like me and a few in between. I loved it!

The Texas League ... been around forever. Our travels would take us to Tulsa, El Paso, Albuquerque, Austin, and Dallas-Ft. Worth. Lots of ballplayers had passed through these towns and I wanted to be one they remembered.

Next morning in the paper, there was my picture and a story about this California hotshot. Well, this was pretty cool; maybe some young Texas beauties would see it and be curious enough to come out to the ballpark.

My dad was on his way with my car. This was not going to be a five-to-a-room-and-no-wheels year. Dave Adlesh, our catcher from Long Beach, talked about living together. It didn't take long to find a nice apartment, two bedrooms, on the west side of town. Hell, I was making big money this year; $650 a month, so it was time to step up.

My dad got there for opening night. Great to see him. The smile on his face let me know just how proud he was. With the ceremonial first pitch over, we took the field. The National Anthem played, the wind blew and the air stunk. Across from Potter County Stadium was the stockyards and when the wind came out of the north, well, it affected attendance. It didn't affect my performance. I had a great night, a few hits, including a home run. I didn't let the press down.

My dad stayed a few days, enjoying every minute. Dave and I got moved in and then it was off on the road. We packed our bags, and this time a beautiful new Greyhound pulled up. The doors opened and there was our driver. He was perfect. Crisp, sharp, official uniform. R.E. Bolmer, he proudly announced as the bus door opened. Load 'em up and let's go kick some ass in Tulsa.

There is so much to learn, not only on the field but off. Everybody has their favorite seat on the bus. You've got those veterans that immediately go to the back to play cards. The skipper always sits in the first seat. Where else? Some are readers, some are dreamers and then there are the sleepers. Me, I was a dreamer. Going down the highway, thinking of where I've already been and sometimes wondering where the hell this is all going to take me. We pulled up to the Adams Hotel in Tulsa a few hours before we would be leaving for the ballpark. Not a bad hotel, not a Dubuque dump, but AA at best.

The bus always leaves about three hours before the game. As we cruised into "Oiler Field," once again the thrill of seeing another ballpark. This one was painted in red, white and blue. When I got off the bus, I felt like I should salute the damn thing. Just out of habit, I always walked out to take a look at the battlefield. Can't tell you why, but something about the green grass …

It was that first night in Tulsa that I learned about a baseball tradition. I noticed that during the national anthem, there were just a few players in our dugout, mostly the young ones. Wasn't until the next night I realized why. I was a little late getting ready and when I bolted from the clubhouse under the grandstands, there were about a dozen of my upstanding teammates under the stands, looking straight up. As the anthem began, they started scurrying around, trying to be as quiet as field mice. What the hell is going on? Then it revealed itself. "Beaver shooting" at its finest. A Tulsa tradition.

It didn't take long to realize the quality of ball was certainly better. I continued my good start in Tulsa, having a real good series. The only problem I was having was getting any validation out of our manager. He kind of had this, "I'll make out the lineup and you guys play," attitude.

That all changed when we started to lose a few games. Shit started flying in the clubhouse; he'd be in your face in the dugout calling you worthless. It turned out this was going to be Lou's last season and he seemed like he wanted it to be simple, carefree and low key. Well, Lou, surprise! That's not what you're going to get.

You can never predict the makeup of a team. We had Ray "Spot" Cordeiro from Rhode Island, left-handed pitcher, about 35 years old. Don Brady, right-hander from somewhere in Texas, about the same age. Leo Posada, power-hitting outfielder and perennial minor leaguer from the Dominican Republic, and several others that were more suspects than prospects. Mixed in were guys on the bubble and then a couple of prospects of course, me being one of those. Great guys, but the motivation for most of these was just to hang in there one more year 'til they could find a job outside of baseball. The dream dies hard.

One of the players, Jim Mahoney, a veteran infielder, was sure spending a lot of time with me. Great guy, been around for years. I'm pretty sure Lou just assigned him to me so he wouldn't have to deal with another prospect. You have to wonder why Lou was even there. Baseball is the good-old-boy network and it's who you know, so I'm sure Lou over the years had earned one final year. He just wanted it to be simple.

As the season went on, I was on fire. Hitting the ball hard, showing power, driving in runs and having a lot of fun. Life off the field was even starting to pick up. My roommate, Dave Adlesh, our catcher, wasn't big on doing anything after the game but going back to the apartment and drinking some Cutty Sark. I, however, started to wander out.

Amarillo was not a big town, but there had to be somewhere to go. The "Reveler," a club downtown, was where the veterans and visiting team were hanging out. Kind of country, smoky and lots of beer drinking. Then I met her. Short, cute, tight jeans and breasts larger than Ethiopia. My god, I just wanted to weigh them.

The next night, I went 0-for-4 and made an error. Lou was in my face after the game. "Stay away from that goddamn Reveler Club, kid. There's no hits in the pussy that hangs out there." What an intelligent way to put it.

Oh well, the season went on. Have you ever been in Albuquerque on a Sunday afternoon? Shit, it's quiet. After the game, nothing was open and all I could do was sit outside the hotel and watch the license plates that went by on Route 66.

Now, Austin, that was a different story. The University of Texas and Schultz's Beer Garden. We stayed at the Driscoll Hotel, right in the middle of town. The Driscoll provided me with another one of those life lessons of being a minor leaguer. Guys were having great success meeting young ladies, or some not so young, but willing. For some reason, the game here was scout the halls, mark the doors where a couple went in and then out the windows and shimmy around fire escapes and ledges to watch the action. Great sport, this beaver shooting.

One night at the Inn of Six Flags, our "road home" when we played the Dallas-Ft. Worth Spurs, it all came to end. About a half dozen of us were in a room - some in plain sight, some behind the drapes and in the closets - watching one of our left-handers in action. A loud knock on the door, then suddenly we were raided. The skipper was not happy when he was awakened at 2:00 AM to find out an orgy was going on, with "peeping toms." We were asked to leave the hotel immediately.

We packed and then sat on the bus until around 5:00. Lou got on, screaming at us. "You low class bunch of perverts. Thank god this is it for me." Next stop, a dump in Ft. Worth, the only place that would take us at that hour.

We started to drop in the standings. Jim Mahoney was constantly reminding me to do my job and not get caught up in it. Things went from bad to worse. We hadn't scored a run in eight games. Our general manager advertised "guaranteed run night." If we don't score a run, the fans would get in free the next day. Guess who the fans were rooting for? Tough to play when the hometown boos you for getting a hit, or catching a ball.

A few of us were sick of this slump, so we decided to flood the field in the middle of the night, just so we could miss a game. This was not an original idea, but it worked. We left town and hit the road for the final stretch. My stats were strong, even if the team's weren't.

Back to Tulsa, one more time. Bus rides could be long and boring. You mainly sleep, read, daydream or play cards. I liked to just stare out the window and daydream. Then it happened, a bus rider's dream. A convertible Mustang pulled up alongside. I couldn't believe my eyes. "Hey, wake up, look at this." Everybody shifted to the left side of the bus. The top was down and so were the driver's pants. He was getting a blow job. He had a big smile on his face. We opened the windows and yelled and screamed. That ended his little fun. Boy, was she pissed. He flipped us off and drove on down the road. Can you imagine how funny our bus looked, going down the highway leaning? What a sight.

When we arrived in Tulsa, we were all pumped up. The Oilers were in the pennant race, and we decided we would love to just kick their ass. With a beaver stop under the bleachers for some final inspiration, we went out and swept the series. Back to Amarillo to wrap up the season. It's amazing what a blow job can do for a team.

I'm Doing Great, Having A Ball – And Then

One day, we were in the middle of infield practice, when suddenly from the dugout emerged Paul Richards, the Astros' General Manager. He held his hand up to Lou at home plate and walked across the infield directly at me. He was holding a batting helmet in his hand. Slowly, he approached and stopped right in my face. "Son, we got a guy in Houston that can play this position." He handed me the helmet and told me to get out in right field.

That was it. Norm Miller was being moved to the outfield. I guess the helmet showed a lot of confidence about my ability to catch a fly ball. I didn't say a word, this man was really intimidating, so off I went and so did he. That night was so strange. I had never been in the outfield, except for the time early in the year in the Astrodome as a guinea pig. Fortunately, nothing came my way that night.

Surprised Again

Then I walked in the clubhouse after the game. Mahoney told me Lou wanted to see me.

"Sit down son. You know you've had a pretty good year, so I told Paul they ought to call you up for the last couple of weeks of the big-league season. So pack 'em up tonight and join the club in LA on Tuesday." So, in one night I went from being a second baseman to an outfielder and from a Sonic to an Astro. I walked back into the locker room in shock.

Mahoney came up and asked if Lou said he recommended to Paul Richards that they take me up. I said, yeah. Jim said, "He does that every year; son of a bitch always wants credit. Your talent is what's getting you there and don't forget that. Great going kid."

I gave Jim a hug and all the guys came up to congratulate me. You feel so fucking unbelievable to be going to the big leagues. At the same time, here are guys that have never gotten close in years and they're truly are happy for you. Just a great game, baseball.

I went home and piled all my shit in the trunk and called home. This is a once-in- a-lifetime call. "Hey, Dad, I've been called up. That's right and I'm joining the team in LA on Tuesday. I'm leaving right now, so I'll see you soon." Route 66 headed west, going to the big leagues at 19 years old. You don't ever forget that.

The Big-League Dream Comes True – For Now

It was great to pull into my parents' driveway on Monday. So much to catch up on before joining the Astros on Tuesday at none other than Dodger Stadium. I can only imagine their feelings.

After a couple of home-cooked meals, it was time to take that drive east to Dodger Stadium, 30 minutes from home. Made it many times, but this was the first as a Major League Player. Naturally, my dad was with me. Mom would come later with the cast of many friends and relatives. I felt older, well traveled, since my last time at the stadium. It's amazing what two years on your own will do for your maturity. Dad and I camouflaged our apprehension with chit chat. We stopped at the gate and I informed the guard I was joining the Astros and if he needed proof, I could show him my equipment bag in the trunk. "No sir, that's fine, and good luck to you." I headed to the players' parking lot, where I rightfully belonged. Into the stadium, Irv in tow. I don't really know if my feet were touching the ground, but my dad did have a hard time keeping up.

There it was, the "Visitors' Door." I opened the "pearly gates." The team hadn't arrived yet, but we were greeted by the clubhouse attendant. "Beau James, son, welcome to the big leagues. You must be Miller. If you need anything, just let me know. Now, your locker is right this way." If you wrote this scene of my dad and me following Beau James, it would have to be titled "The Pride and the Passion." There it was; my name in the slot, uniform on the hook. Number 21. Wow, I've come a long way from number 76 in spring training.

Shortly after, the team came rolling in. A few faces had been added, and some subtracted, during the season. Guys came by to shake my hand or slap me on the ass. They were great to my dad. There was a slight sense I had gained some respect since leaving the Astrodome five months earlier, and going out and putting up some good AA stats. The atmosphere was lively, even though it was not the best of seasons for the ballclub. But in baseball, everyday is literally a new day for the team - and for each and every individual. So, optimism always seems to be the feeling of the day.

There was plenty of time to get dressed and take in all the sights and sounds. It was different from the spring training atmosphere. Obviously, a lot nicer locker room, but this was it, the fucking big leagues, and I was soaking it all in. My dad thought it was time for him to go out to the stands; I really think he was just overwhelmed. We shook hands and off he went. As he walked by the ice cream cooler, Beau James opened it up and said, "Mr. Miller, have an ice cream on me." My dad reached in and grabbed a popsicle. "Welcome to the bigs, Mr. Miller." That smile on my dad's face will never be forgotten.

I was summoned into the manager's office. Luman Harris was sitting at his desk as I walked in. He stood up and extended his hand. "Good work, son, you had a hell of a year."

"Thanks."

"I understand we're moving you to the outfield?"

"Well it looks that way."

"I don't think Morgan is going to be giving up the second base job any time soon."

"I guess not, sir."

"Well, here's what I want you to do. I'm not going to play you, doesn't look good when you throw a rookie out there against a team in the pennant race."

"Yes, sir, I understand."

"This is your hometown right?"

"Yep."

"Well, you just make sure mom and dad and all those friends see you before the game, then you take a seat way down at the other end of the dugout. Just watch and learn and stay out of the way."

So, I headed back to my locker. The Turk and the Bear were waiting. "What the fuck you doing up here?" I'm telling you, these guys could intimidate a mass fucking murderer. Before I could respond, the two nut buckets were gone.

It was time for batting practice, so I threw on the number 21 and headed down the tunnel. I was on the visiting team, but it sure felt familiar to walk onto the field that sunny afternoon. I ran out toward second base and then remembered: "outfield; you're now an outfielder," so I just kept going to center field to shag. Pitchers were hitting first, then the extra men, followed by the lineup. I was told that once season was over, I would get a short break and then be off to Arizona to learn how to play the outfield. So, I roamed the outfield in the beautiful green grass of Dodger Stadium.

We didn't have our names on uniforms back then, and I wondered if number 21 would be in the scorecards for all my friends to see. Ah, let the ego begin.

I jumped in the cage and felt great. I mean, no pressure, I hit .290 with 20 home runs at Amarillo, and I wasn't playing that night, as told sternly by the skipper. The fans were arriving, and I couldn't help but notice my entourage start to arrive. I could see my mom had found my dad; she was pointing towards me to everyone. I waved; what the hell, it *was* Mom.

When the Dodgers took the field, I hung out a little near the batting cage, just to see some of my idols, like Tommy Davis, Maury Wills and maybe get a close look at Sandy Koufax and Don Drysdale. Then, back up to the clubhouse.

It was game time, so down to the bench for my first big-league game. I headed far down the bench, as instructed. It was a close game; Claude Osteen, a left-hander, was on the mound for the Dodgers. We were heading into the ninth inning. "Miller, get a bat." I heard it, but we had to have another Miller, I thought, because I was clearly told that being a rookie, I had no chance to get in this one. "Miller, let's go, son." I glanced to my left and they were looking right at me and waving. I stumbled down to the bat rack. "Get up there, son, get something started." I grabbed the first bat I got my hands on and stepped onto the field. I noticed they were waiting for me up at home plate, so I didn't even stop to loosen up or get some pine tar on the bat. As I got closer to home plate, the umpire glanced at me and said, "Welcome to the big leagues." That was nice, I thought. As I was ready to step into the batter's box, the umpire tapped me on the shoulder. I turned and he gazed through his mask. "Son, it's a lot easier to hit up here without a jacket on." My teammates were on the dugout floor, laughing. No wonder my name hadn't been announced yet. How do you walk up to home plate your first time in the bigs and take a jacket off, without losing your cool? You don't!

Then I heard it. "Now hitting, number 21, Norm Miller." Screams came from the stands; my mom's was the loudest. I stepped into the batter's box, shaking from head to toe. How many times had I dreamed of this moment; and for it to be happening in my home town was too much to bear. The lefthander, Osteen, delivered the first pitch and paralysis had set in. Strike one. Never had I felt so petrified. Strike two. I stepped out of the box, trying to prevent hyperventilation. Then, low and away for a ball, followed by an inside fastball that just missed. The count even up at two and two. I stepped out of the box, took several deep breaths and decided that I would somehow swing at the next pitch, no matter what. Osteen let it go, and somehow the ball found my bat. A line drive up the middle. I stood there in disbelief. Screams came from the dugout. "Run, run." Shit, I was almost thrown out at first base. There I was, standing on the bag, when Wes Parker, the first baseman, came over to hold me on. They held up the game and retrieved the ball for me; the first-hit tradition. I looked at Wes Parker and shook his hand. "Hi, Norm Miller." He didn't know what to do. I looked across the field at coach Busby. Was that the steal sign? Osteen took his stretch, looked over at me and then I was gone. I slid into second and Maury Wills put the tag down. Safe! I shook Maury's hand; hell, I may never get out here again, so I just wanted to meet all my idols. I was stranded at second.

I returned to the dugout in a coma. I had just gotten my first big-league hit. This was the biggest moment of my young life.

After the game, the baseball was delivered to my locker. It had been inscribed, "Norm Miller, first big-league hit." We had lost the game, but I got a lot of congratulations from my teammates. They had all been in my shoes at one time or another.

When I left the clubhouse and met my family and friends, it was overwhelming. My mom still couldn't get a grasp on just what had happened. I was a hero. My dad, being my dad, shook my hand and just smiled. "Come on, let's go eat and celebrate." The team was allowing me to stay at home with the folks, so we headed to Hamburger Hamlet out by our home. My friends surprised me with a cake with one candle on it. I was starting to come down to earth when none other than Don Drysdale walked up to our table.

"Congratulations, son! I'll see you down the road." Now, how unbelievable is that? Don Drysdale, one of the greatest, at my table, shaking my hand. The irony is that we went to the same high school. When I had sat in the goddamn vice principal's office a few years earlier for detention, I had to look at Drysdale's picture on the wall. The Vice Principal made a point to tell me every day. "You won't make it like big Don. He went to class." Hey, Mr. Comerford, fuck you.

I didn't make it on the field the next two games and we were off to St. Louis. As you move up the food chain of baseball, the differences are describable. "A-Ball" is young kids learning to play the game every day in small towns around America. You're making more money than most your age, but it's not about that. You travel on buses that have seen many miles, and you stay in hotels that don't leave the light on. In AA, the quality of play is tougher. You continue to refine the fundamentals and work on what will get you to the next level. The money is a little more, but the expenses are, too. So are the expectations. The towns are a little bigger and the buses faster. But the Major League, now that's a huge jump. "Indescribable."

I Should Have Stayed On The Bus

After that final game in LA, I packed my bag and that was it. You hop on a charter bus to the airport where you don't even see the terminal. Onto a charter jet and off you go. We landed in St. Louis in the early morning hours. The bus was waiting on the tarmac and we were off to the Chase Park Plaza Hotel, a beautiful hotel on the outskirts of the city. The room keys are waiting and your luggage is delivered shortly after you arrive in the room. Nineteen years old and I'm discovering first class - and loving it. Another great thing was the meal money which went from $6.00 in AA to $18.00. I just got hungrier. My salary, which had been $650.00 a month at Amarillo, and we were paid only for five months out of the year in the minor leagues, was bounced up for the last couple of weeks of the major-league season to be at the rate of $7,500 per season, which was the major-league minimum. So those last couple of weeks I was going to see about as much as I had made all year.

The hours of ballplayers are ass backwards from most folks. Here it was 5:30 AM or so and we were just getting to bed. The bus to the ballpark was to leave the hotel three hours before game time. So while most people are asleep, we're traveling. When most people are working, we're sleeping.

St. Louis, Missouri, a real baseball town. Legends such as Dizzy Dean, Stan "The Man" Musial and many others. So much tradition. The bus pulled up to Sportsman's Park. This was the last year for the old park; the Cardinals were going to be moving into a new stadium downtown. I just followed the other guys, through the gates, down the halls and into the old clubhouse. The hair stood on the back of my neck just thinking of whose steps I was following in. I wondered if I would ever get over those feelings. I hoped not.

I was a rookie; to be seen and not heard. Follow the leaders. The socks and jocks come on, put on your Rawlings cleats and down another tunnel. Sportsman's Park had the classic, old-time look. Dark green, wood seats, non-symmetrical, big scoreboard; just a work of art in my mind. Stepping onto the field, the 180-degree view came to life. I took it all in and went about the business of fitting in.

Around the batting cage, I saw a couple of guys I played against in Tulsa. The Cardinals had called them up for a sneak-peak of life in the bigs. I went over and said hi. There was a comfort level of being able to stand, bat in hand, and talk to other "big leaguers." You know, that feeling like you belong. The chit chat was cut short when I was reminded about fraternizing with the other team. Once the fans are in the stands, the league doesn't want you to be talking to opponents. I thought, shit, I gotta talk to somebody, and my own players haven't exactly opened their arms yet. I was wondering if the Cardinal rookies were having the same thoughts.

The next morning I was in the hotel coffee shop having breakfast at the counter. My waitress, very cute, struck up a conversation. She wanted to know if I was a ballplayer. I responded proudly.

I got my first major-league start that night. When I saw my name on the lineup card, the nerves came to attention. I almost didn't know how to act. You dream of moments like this. I had barely recovered from my first major-league hit. Also, I was going to be in left field, where I had never played before. Oh, and a left hander is throwing, Ray Sadecki. Gagging is not allowed before the game; I had to do my best to hide my fear and anxiety.

Grabbing my bat, getting ready to face the crafty left-hander, as he was always described on TV; Coach Busby told me sinker, slider, keeps the ball down. Okay, I got it. This time I did make a stop in the on-deck circle. Some pine tar, swing the lead bat, check to make sure my jacket wasn't still on, and up to home plate I strolled. Three hours later, I was 0-for-4, looked terrible against those sinkers and sliders and looked like a clown in left field, surrounding a couple of fly balls, barely catching them. It wasn't pretty. It was memorable for me; I hope nobody else. I had seen sinkers and sliders before, these just seemed different, I thought, as I was getting dressed after the game. I did manage to get a couple of "hang in theres" from the guys, which helped. First on the bus, I was still trying to figure out what happened.

There was a tap on the window, I turned and saw a smiling, recognizable face. It was my waitress from the hotel. I slid the window down. She asked if I would like to get something to eat. I didn't think about rules or what to do; I was hungry and companionship always brings me out of slumps.

I bolted from the bus before anyone else showed. We got in her car and she asked if I had ever been to Gas Light Square. "No, can't say that I have." Ages hadn't been established yet; I only hope she doesn't take me to a bar. Gas Light Square was different, quaint, lined with bars and restaurants. Sure enough, we parked and walked like we were on a mission. Into the corner bar we went. I just knew I was about to be asked for ID. Nope, I guess I looked older in my blue blazer, and the tie sure helped.

That she was not a rookie at this place also probably helped me get a pass. Several gin and tonics later, it was time to get back to the hotel. Being late for curfew after just a few games in the bigs wouldn't be too smart. What to do? She handed me the keys and asked me to drive. And wouldn't you know it, the car wouldn't start. We hailed a cab and on our way to the hotel she suggested that I should just come home with her. "I live real close to the Chase and you can take a cab or even walk in the morning." God gave us a brain and a penis and only enough blood to operate one at a time. As the blood rushed from my head, the decision was made.

I knew her name, nothing else. I knew she was good looking, confident and had perky tits. So here we go, up the elevator down the hall and key in door. Curfew had passed so I might as well go for it. The room was dark, a candle was lit. Small but nicely furnished. Clean, but oh my god, what the fuck is that baby doing on the bed? Oh, shit, who is this? She hands a young girl some cash. There I was, a mother and daughter and me. This was new. She did everything to relieve me of the tenseness that had overcome my body. The baby was put in her crib, and then we kissed. Suddenly no more 0-for-4, no curfew, it was ten times worse.

"Quick, grab your stuff," the sliding glass door opened to a patio. "Get out now." As I picked up my loafers, the sound of a key in the door put a rocket up my ass. I flew out onto the patio. Shaking from fear, not the 40-degree night, I just knew I had to get out of there. I looked over the railing and saw my escape. I threw my loafers, blazer and tie over the railing. I shimmied down the drain pipe right into some hedges, grabbed my stuff and bolted.

It is 2:30 AM, I'm in St. Louis somewhere; which way to the Chase Park Plaza? I will never do this again. I stopped a cab and told him to drop me off around from the entrance. I found a back door open. I went through the kitchen, raced up the stairs to the second floor. Then took the elevator up to my floor. I was safe, the adventure was over.

The phone woke me up early. A low voice told me to lay low. "Don't answer your phone. He's wearing a beige topcoat and gray slacks. By the way, do you have my car keys?" What the fuck, I thought. I checked my blazer and there they were.

"Yeah, I've got them."

"Put them in an envelope, call the bellman and have them sent down to the restaurant. Just stay in your room."

Holy shit, I'm fucking dead. The phone rang a couple of times that day. I didn't get near it. Room service was the order of the day. The other good thing, I thought, it was get-away day and I would just send my luggage down and wait 'til the last moment to board the bus. If he was going to get me, it would be with a rifle shot in the dugout.

It was time, 4:55 PM, I jumped in the elevator. The doors open, lobby level. I look out and there is nobody with a knife in their hand waiting. I calmly head towards the exit of the lobby and out of the corner of my eye, I see beige topcoat, with gray slacks on the house phone. I picked up the pace, jumped on the bus and off it went. Great timing.

I didn't start that night. We won and I didn't have to leave the dugout. As the plane lifted off the runway, I waved good-bye to St. Louis. Nice town.

The final week and a half of being a major leaguer didn't go quite as well as I hoped. To be honest, I was just over-matched. The harder I tried when I got in, the worse it got. The game just seemed faster than in the minors. The pitchers found my weaknesses and I think they sent out a scouting report around the league. "Pitch him inside with hard stuff. He likes it out over the plate."

Put The Helmet Back On

I was going home to California for the winter and just prior to leaving, Paul Richards called me in. He wanted me to go to Arizona for several weeks to get a head start on learning the outfield. They were delegating the coaching duties to a player coach from Amarillo, Leo Posada. That was great with me. Leo and I had hit third and fourth all year in Amarillo and had a great relationship. I was 19 and Leo was baseball old. That is, he was in his mid thirties and never had been in the big leagues. He knew the game and he could hit the fastball, but it was that fucking breaking stuff that held him back.

Just before my short break at home with mom and dad, I was voted the top second baseman in AA by Topps bubblegum. The irony, I'm on my way to Scottsdale to learn how to play another position. That's the game, anything at anytime can change.

The previous year, I was an Angel making double plays, now I'm an Astro catching flies. To some, I guess, changing positions would be tough, especially after being honored for my past play. But in reality it was the best for me. I went to Scottsdale with a good attitude and besides, I realized that I was getting the shit kicked out of me on a lot of double plays. Paul Richards was right, "Got to get rid of the ball quicker."

I had two major problems that Leo explained to me. One, I had to stop running on my heels; it makes the fly ball appear to jump around like a knuckle ball. The other goal was to develop a much stronger arm. Every day, we spent hours at the park. Fly ball to my left, fly ball to my right. "Get on the balls of your feet and the flies won't jump around so much," he kept yelling. The day finally came that Leo allowed me to take off the helmet. In the meantime, we played long catch every day and by the end of the month of training, I could throw. Leo told me he was going to recommend to the club that they might want to put me in right field, where I was more comfortable. That was a nice way of saying you're brutal in left. I guess always being on the right side of the infield was where I was comfortable and with improved arm strength, right field could be my position.

We parted ways; what a great coach. I had new-found confidence and couldn't wait for spring training to start. In January, the annual letter and contract arrived. I would once again be going to spring training with the big club and projected to play at AAA, Oklahoma City. I packed and pumped up to get back to Cocoa Beach.

A New Year And A Funny Roommate

Arriving back for the second year was so much easier. I knew what to expect and was ready to show how much I had improved. For some reason when I checked in, I had a room to myself, but it wasn't going to last long.

Camp was underway when a young kid was brought into the clubhouse. Red haired, freckle faced and strong looking. He walked up to Bob Aspromonte, the regular third baseman, and told him he was going to get his job. This confident young man was Doug Rader, a product of Wesleyan University out of the Chicago area. At the end of the day, I had a new roommate.

At least I had someone my own age. Not that I didn't enjoy my time with Bill Heath the prior camp, but there was a slight generation gap. Doug was something else from day one. I got up and gargled my Micron one morning and it about killed me. Aqua Velva had found its way into the wrong bottle. Doug liked that. Another night, I was in a playful mood so I climbed on top of the closet and waited for him to come in the room. When he did, I leaped from the ledge onto his back.

He put me into an "airplane spin" and slammed me down on my bed breaking all the slats. He liked that, too. I realized that I was no match for Doug, so I just stayed on the defensive the rest of the camp.

I spent most of the camp continuing to improve in the outfield. The games I did get in, however, were mostly in left. The Astros had Rusty Staub, quite a ballplayer, in right and he liked to play every day. Left field was still a problem for me. Several times I heard, "Put a tent over that guy, it looks like a circus out there." But I kept working and the other thing I already knew was that I would be heading directly to Okie City to play for Mel McGaha and the 89er's.

I wished Doug luck; he was off to Durham in the Carolina league. I knew he would do great and Durham was really going to enjoy this guy. AAA, here I come.

Big In Oklahoma

8 9er stadium was good looking. Located at the fairgrounds, it was newer and bigger than Davenport and Amarillo. The town's reputation was "great place to play." We would be playing in Tulsa, which had moved up from the Texas League; cool, more beaver shooting. Albuquerque also had made the jump. Then there was San Diego, Seattle, Tacoma, Vancouver B.C., Spokane, Phoenix, Indianapolis and Hawaii. This was not a bus league anymore. We would be flying just about everywhere.

Once again, I was the youngest at 20. A few other prospects, a couple of suspects and some cagey veterans. Expectations at this level were high. You're only one step from the top and it's time to perform at a much higher level against tough competition.

Mel McGaha called me into his office. I was going to be moved to right field. I had played several "B" games in spring training for Mel and liked him. Big man, southern drawl, more on the quiet side. He laid out what he expected. Learn from my mistakes, listen to the coaches, and watch my temper (which was another way of saying "grow up"). I had been known to occasionally throw a bat or helmet or a fit when things didn't go just right.

I knew most of the guys on this club. It's a different world, the minor leagues. There are so many teams at different levels and only so many prospects. For those guys that love the game, they just move around as long as somebody will give them a job. They also, in the back of their minds, think maybe, just maybe, I can get a shot. One day in the bigs was all they wanted.

The crowds were great in Oklahoma City. On a good night, we would have four or five thousand fans. On special days, like "Cow Milking Contest Day," we would pack them in. Maybe six thousand would come.

Another great feature in Oklahoma City was a club called the "The 10th Inning Club," located just down the block from the stadium. The proprietor, Frank Ross, and his girlfriend catered to the players. Kind of a dive, but Frank's scouting reports on the girls circulating in the room were dead-on. I'm still underage, but I'm an 89er and that gives me rights. My dad had once again brought my car to town and stayed for a few games. In fact, he was invited to ride the bus to Tulsa with the team. What a thrill for him and me. Another thrill about Tulsa was the National Anthem tradition. This I didn't share with Irv. I'm not sure he would like having a pervert for a son.

AAA ball is great. The cities are big, the press coverage great and I was certainly getting my share of it early in the year in Okie City. They were playing up the role of being from California, driving around town in my new car. Keep it coming. It also helped that I got off to a good start at the plate and my defensive skills had vastly improved. We were also winning more than we were losing. I managed to find a nice apartment with Tom Griffin, right-handed pitcher from my home town. Tom, a year or so younger, was a rising star. Great fastball and tremendous slider.

It wasn't long before the downside of playing in Oklahoma City revealed itself. Weather! Holy shit, out of nowhere, storms would roll in and we had to take cover in the clubhouse, which looked like a fortress. One minute the skies were clear, a wind blowing out to left, and then, boom. Skies would darken, the winds would pick up and people would scatter. Let's get on the road.

Everything about the Coast League was nicer. We didn't fly first class or anything, but instead of those god-awful, nine-hour bus trips, a few hours on a turbo-prop or whatever we took, was a welcome relief. Of course, many complained about things, but that's the nature of spoiled ballplayers. Hotels were a notch up, meal money a few dollars more and the women nicer looking, some even had all their teeth. The one trip we all looked forward to was later in the season, Hawaii. We would play a five-game series there, so I had that one circled for sure.

I suddenly had another curve ball thrown at me. The Vietnam War was in full swing and the club had a chance to get a few of us into the Army Reserves. So with about an hour's notice, I had to hop on Braniff Airlines and get down to Houston to be inducted into the Army Reserve. Once inducted, I would have to attend scheduled meetings in Houston. I was told that it would be some time before I would have to go to basic training. That was good news. I would miss a lot of games because of the meetings, but I wouldn't miss the whole season. Yes, some get all the breaks.

Playing every day is not easy. This is something that makes you understand the point of why baseball, unlike other major sports, has a minor-league system. But it can take its toll. In high school you played a couple games a week. In college maybe four games a week and a 60-game schedule. Now it's two months of spring training, 100-plus game schedule with lots of travel, double headers on Sundays and it's for a living. You have to learn how to deal with playing every day. The physical and mental aspect of the game. The pressure of learning the game. It's nothing you can prepare for.

We were in Phoenix right in the middle of summer. I had played every game and on this particular day we had a double header. Hot took on a new meaning for this double dip. Between games, we tried to cool down in the freezing locker room. I waited 'til the last moment to go out for the second game. I was leading off, so I just went right from the cool to the steaming heat at home plate. I stepped in the batter's box and promptly passed out. Just dropped right on home plate. The umpire made the call, "He's out!" That little episode, diagnosed as total exhaustion brought on by dehydration, put me on the bench for a few days. Of course, the compassionate players started to question my manhood within hours. So, those four or five days off were good for my physical being but not good on the mental being. "Have a nice rest today, pussy. How's she feeling today? Oh, do you still have your period?" Anyway, what in normal life would have been a week's vacation was cut short. I couldn't take the harassment so I begged Mel to let me back in the lineup.

Another thing about moving up in baseball is you always see someone on their way down. On a trip to San Diego to play the Missions, I thought I recognized one of their players. I couldn't put a name with a face until I heard his name as he stepped up to the plate in the first inning. "Now hitting, Bobby DelGreco." I was in right field and I couldn't believe my ears. Bobby fuckin' DelGreco. Former Hollywood Star from my childhood, a guy I just loved to watch. I wanted to call time out and run in to shake his hand. The next day I came out early, just to find him. This was an early boyhood idol. I saw him standing by the batting cage. I walked up and just stared at him.

"What's up, son?"

"Mr. DelGreco, when I was a kid, you were my favorite with the Stars." I think the "kid" part of the statement was not appreciated. But just as I always thought, he was a great guy. We chatted a few minutes; he was now at least 40 years old and still swinging it. For me, that was really a cool moment in my young career. I wanted to ask him why he was still doing it, but just watching him step in the cage, I understood. He could still swing the bat and that kind of answered the question for me.

As the games clicked off, we were getting closer to the big trip to Hawaii. A lot of the guys had made the trip and their excitement to return was infectious. "You'll love it, Miller. We stay on the beach and it's great. Hard bellies everywhere, the sun and surf and we get to wear shorts to the ballpark."

We stepped off the plane and immediately had a team picture taken next to the airplane surrounded by beautiful Hawaiian dancers. Off to the hotel for a five-game road trip. Howie Reed, a veteran pitcher, asked if I wanted to go for a walk around Waikiki. "Sure, let's do it." What Howie really meant was let's go get a Mai Tai. Within minutes we were sipping Mai Tais at the International Village. I should have stopped at one. Howie, being starting pitcher, had nothing to worry about as he held me up walking back to the hotel. I was shit-faced. I stumbled onto the bus, Mel as always in the front seat. I snuck by him, bouncing off seats, working my way back to the back of the bus.

We arrived at the ballpark; I found my locker and just was blasted. How the hell am I going to do this? It didn't take long to get exposed. Right field was just 250 feet down the line. The first hitter took a low and away pitch and hit a line drive to right. I took two steps in and threw up in my glove, but it was too late. I took it right on the forehead and went down like a rock. Time was called. Mel and the trainer came out and I guess the fumes told the story. They dragged me right to the locker room and left me for the duration of the game. By game's end, I was pretty much coherent. To make things worse, we got killed that game. While I had been drinking, some of the other players had gone body surfing. A drunk and tired team. As Mel stood in the middle of the clubhouse screaming, it was clear the next four days in Hawaii would consist of eating, resting and we better win the next three or we might be paddling home.

There always seem to be one or two special fans in every town. In Okie City we had Chester. Middle-aged guy, not sure what Chester did, other than come to every game and sit out near the bullpen in the grandstands. I never asked about Chester; would just wave to him when I saw him. Mel told me he was going to give me a rare night off. So I thought, hell, I'm going to go sit out in the bullpen with the guys. A few innings into the game, Chester asked if I would like some cold grapefruit juice. "Sure." He passed me a large cup through a hole in the fence. Hot summer night, got the night off; the juice tasted great. Couple of innings later: "Hey, Norm want some more?

"Sure, Chester, this shit's great."

Around the eighth inning, I started going blind. I didn't know what was wrong, but the numbers on the scoreboard in left field were all blurry. Someone was yelling from the dugout for me. I stood up and - whoa! - fell back on the bullpen bench. Guys started laughing. I tried to get up as the yelling continued from the dugout. I finally, with a shove, got up and headed into the dugout. "Get a bat, you're pinch hitting," Mahoney said.

I grabbed a bat, totally aware of my problem, but just trying to not let Mel see me stumble. I took big steps out of the dugout, took a couple of swings with the lead bat and approached home plate. I heard my name announced and knew it was time to step in the box. I looked out toward the mound and realized, I am shit faced drunk and blind. I turned towards the catcher and told him, "Give me three fastballs, but please keep them outside." He said "Chester's still in the bullpen with that white lightning shit." I swung at two outside fastballs and when I heard the call, "strike three," I was thrilled. Chester was banished for the rest of the season and it cost me another $100 and a private meeting with Mel.

Jerked Out Of The Lineup And Told To Get A Haircut

A few weeks later, I was in the batter's box at Indianapolis, listening to the National Anthem. When it was over, I started to head up to home plate. A whistle came from the dugout and Mel was signaling me to come back. As I reached the dugout, he said, "Go inside you're not playing tonight."

"What do you mean I'm not playing?"

"Just get your ass in the clubhouse and I'll be up there in a minute." Whoa, he's pissed. What the hell did I do? I was at the infamous Rat Fink Club the night before, but nothing happened.

I sat there in my locker and then Mel came in. He was a great guy unless you fuck up. "Pack your bags you're finished here." His expression was serious. I didn't know what to do. I was just shocked and scared. He turned to leave as if that's the end of the story. Then a turn of his head and a big grin. "Hey you're going up to join the club in Atlanta. Jimmy Wynn got hurt and they need another outfielder. Your plane ticket is on the way, so get dressed and good luck. One more thing, you might want to think about getting the hair cut before Grady sees you."

You just never know when you might get caught. Just like your mother always warns you about clean underwear, I was going to Atlanta with hair that would guarantee me a quick return to the minors or at least a lot of grief. Grady Hatton had replaced Luman Harris as manager and he liked the clean-cut look. Not the California "hot dog" look I was sporting.

Upon arriving at the hotel very late, I asked the desk about a barber. I was lucky; there was one in the hotel. I was up early and in the chair.

This trip back to the bigs was not a long stay. Jimmy got better quicker than expected and I was back on my way to AAA. Clean-cut and actually excited in the sense that sitting on the bench is not for me. You never like to see someone come back down, but in this case I think it was pretty well known I was just filling space on the roster.

This turned out to be a tough year. I never really got going and my temper was starting to flare up and get in my way. I was having trouble dealing with all the changes.

The change in position, AAA and those Army Reserve meetings. Every time I seemed to get going with the bat, I had to hop on a plane for meetings in Houston, and then there was a two-week summer camp right in the middle of the season.

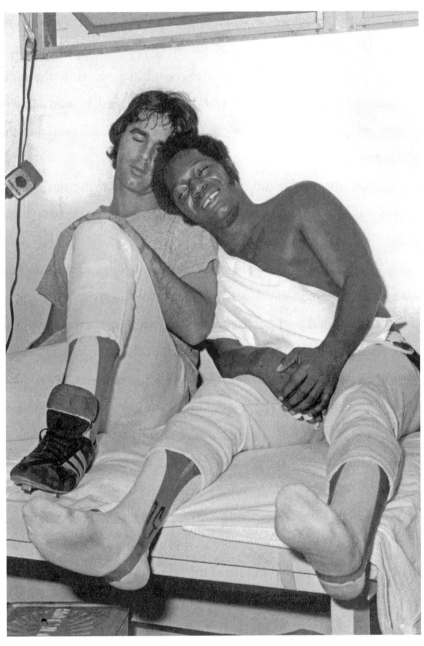

Jimmy Wynn, "The Toy Cannon."

What's he smiling about?

My stats were way off and I was just too damn young to deal with it all. My off-the-field habits were not the best, either. Too much time at the "10th Inning Club," but what the hell, it's a learning process - the minor leagues - and I was sure learning.

I would call my mom and dad every Sunday and try to paint a pretty picture. My mom was more concerned about how I was eating. My dad was always calming. You want to do so well for them, but their understanding was great.

When the season ended, my confidence was at a low for the first time in my life. What did the club think of me now? Was I still a prospect?

The drive west a year earlier was to join the big club. Those miles just clicked away with excitement. This trip, I just kind of cruised down the highway trying to figure it all out.

You know, I thought, I'm only 20 and I had a lot of interruptions during the season. Even though my average dropped from the previous year and my power was down, so were my at-bats by over 200 plate appearances. The drive went on. I kind of messed up a couple of times. I mean, getting led astray in Hawaii with those Mai Tais and taking a line drive in the forehead weren't good. Drinking Chester's magical mix during a game and going blind at home plate wasn't very smart. I wonder if Mel put any of that in his reports.

Boy, it was a long drive home! Bring on 1967.

One of the great things about living in Southern California is you can play baseball year round. There are so many pro ballplayers, we would get together and work out. Also, as spring training approached, we had a team that would play the local colleges. Like the old barnstorming days, one day we'd play USC, another day, UCLA. The college players had no problem getting up for us. We had to worry a little bit about getting hit in the head by some young phenom trying to show us just how hard he could throw. The fans came out and it was lots of fun and good baseball.

Boredom Gets Me In Trouble

The winter months can drag on, especially when you're ready to step up and redeem yourself for the previous year. I couldn't wait. My contract came in the mail and once again I was going to camp with the big club. The letter enclosed was from our new General Manager, Spec Richardson. He said I had a good chance to make the club. Yes, I'm still a prospect.

This would be my fourth spring training. I was starting to feel pressure to stick with the team, even if it was self-imposed. But I had some obstacles called Army duties. Weekend trips to Houston from wherever the team was playing and two weeks of camp in the middle of the season take a toll.

The one thing I was starting to become aware of was change. When you walk in the camp, there are always new faces. Then you hear that so and so is gone. Some get released, maybe traded or retired. In high school, we played with the same kids we grew up with. In professional ball you play with guys you just met. You ride the buses countless hours together telling stories and lies. You have beers and just shoot the shit. I loved this part of the game. After a win or a loss, we would hang out. What you don't realize is that players move from one minor-league team to another probably more than in the big leagues. Sometimes you see them again, but others just vanish.

The routine of spring training can drive you nuts. You spend the first couple of weeks working on the fundamentals. We all bitch and moan about having to do this, but they say a team that isn't bitching about something isn't a team. Then the Grapefruit League starts. Get on a bus, drive across Florida, get off the bus, play a game and then back to Cocoa. You eat dinner and pass out.

The monotony does have to be broken occasionally. As I stood on deck for the start of a game at Cocoa, I noticed a very good looking girl in the front row. Being single and lonely, I walked over and gave her a ball. You know, promote the game. Next time up, she had given the batboy her phone number to give to me. I casually slipped it in my pocket to be utilized later. I hit a home run and tipped my hat as I headed toward the dugout. She smiled again.

Later that night on the roof of her apartment building, we were busted in a very compromising position. Well, I figured, this will fry my ass. First of all, thank god she was of age. Second, when they discovered I was an Astro and I could get them some tickets, things started to look up. Finally, as I sat there at the police station, I learned that this was the mayor's daughter and they were just going to kind of look past this little incident. How lucky can you get? Back to the field of play I went, swearing I'm sticking close to camp from now on.

Be Careful Who You Make Friends With

I was playing in a lot of games this spring. Mostly in left field, again. Very scary out there for me. Fly balls always curve towards the foul lines. I just move better to my right than my left. That's my glove hand and that seems to be the way it is for most outfielders. Rusty Staub was a fixture in right, so I just needed to get used to it and not get killed.

I was getting more comfortable around the big leaguers. Whenever you're invited to go out with them or do anything, it kind of makes you feel like you belong. Wade Blasingame and Denny LeMaster, both left-handed pitchers that came over from the Braves, invited me to go bass fishing after practice one day. Now, I know nada, zip, zero about fishing. However, I did want to be one of the guys. Big mistake. Both Wade and Denny were fisherman types. Denny had brought his bass boat down for camp. We loaded up and started going down the Indian River. The wind kept picking up and the fish were not biting. Denny had a good(?) idea, "Let's look along the banks for snakes." Now, I'm in a bass boat, very narrow. I am petrified of snakes and made the mistake of telling them. So naturally, the hunt took on a new meaning: let's scare the shit out of Norm. Fish we couldn't find; snakes, all over the banks. Not ordinary snakes, but water moccasins. I screamed, begged and probably cried. Then Wade caught a snake on the end of an oar. He held it in the air and I shit. This was the last time these mother fuckers would ever get me out again. Somehow, they realized that I wasn't kidding and as the sun started to go down, we headed in. Horseshit left-handers. I hate them.

The next day, sitting in the clubhouse before our game and feeling humiliated by the "snakemasters," I was suddenly confronted by two men. Not just any men. You learn after a few years the tell-tale signs of what will be defining moments in your career. This was one of them. These two men put the stamp of approval that it is your turn. Having seen them around every spring training about this time, I had watched them go down the rows of lockers doing their thing. I knew what this was about and I was ready. They stared at me and I stared right back. I waited them out. The ongoing story from the previous day no longer mattered. The next words were all I wanted to hear. "Norm, would you please stand up?" We were eye-to-eye, staring at each other. Then it happened. They measured my inseam, my waist and my shoulders. This is big. They had the final roster for the big-league team and I was on it. Custom-make that uniform, boys, and make it tight. This is a great day. The two men from Rawlings have finally stopped at my locker.

But then my dream was shattered. When it came time to break camp, I was told I would be returning to Oklahoma City for a little while. I was told it was because of a roster situation. Well, there's nothing I can do but go where they say and get off to a good start. At least I know my uniform will fit when I get back.

And that's what I did. After the first ten games, I was hitting .406 when I got the call. Back to the Astrodome. I talked with my dad and told him this was it. I'm sticking this time. "Just do your best, swing the bat and listen to your coaches."

Is This The Year?

M y salary was now going to take a jump to $7,500. Time to step up my quality of life. I moved into a motel on Main Street where a lot of the players were staying. The Surrey House was just perfect. Rooms with kitchens, a few blocks from the Astrodome and lots of company. When we went on the road, they stored our stuff so we wouldn't have to pay. Now, this is big league. Time to call dad and get the Chevy down. By the way, I no longer was a four-on-the-floor guy. Now I have a beautiful, maroon Super Sport, with white interior and automatic. Class, pure class.

When I walked in the clubhouse the first person I saw was coach Nellie Fox. As a kid playing second base, he was one of my idols. In spring training he wouldn't say a thing to me. I think it was that "rookie thing," but he gave me a welcoming and patted me on the ass. Nellie Fox, Hall of Famer for sure, and he's acknowledging me. The stars are aligning; this is going to be the year.

I checked out the tight-fitting uniform, perfect. I was called into Grady Hatton's office. "Left field tonight. Good luck." That was about it. Everybody loved Grady Hatton when he managed at Oklahoma City before I got there. What little I had been around him, I couldn't figure out why. Not many words and not many smiles.

As I took my position in left, listening to the National Anthem, watching the exploding scoreboard go off, I had that feeling that this time I "belonged." I'm 21 years old, it's time to live up to expectations. At least mine.

It didn't take long for my first circus catch on a routine fly ball to left. I just hate it out here. I continued to take fly balls everyday from Coach Al Heist, but it just wasn't comfortable.

I was platooning with Ron Davis in left. Now, he could play the position. I'd better hit to stay in the lineup. When you're a young ballplayer, you always feel like you're just one fuck-up away from the minors.

This Shit Is Hard

As the season rolled along, I struggled at the plate. The difference in the big leagues became very obvious to me. The pitchers could spot your weaknesses very quickly. Everybody started pitching me inside and jamming me. I'm the type of hitter that likes the ball out over the plate and these guys knew that. So I started to adjust. I moved off-plate a little. Then I started seeing a lot of balls on the outside part of the plate. In the minors you might have one guy on each opposing team that could put it where he wanted. But in the bigs, these guys could throw any pitch at any time where they wanted it. I started to really press and things just got worse.

The team was not playing well and Grady was fit to be tied. This made it even tougher. I tried to keep my confidence up but I was over-matched most nights. In the minors I had some power, but playing in the spacious Dome, my power was diminished by the size of the field. I hit a lot of deep flies that would be home runs in the minor-league parks but were routine fly balls in the big leagues.

Night after night, facing guys like Gaylord Perry and his "spit ball," Juan Marichal, who didn't know there was a middle of the plate, Ferguson Jenkins, who could pinpoint that slider on the outside corner - the list just goes on and on. Then you get to try and battle Don Drysdale. Joe Morgan, our second baseman, told me before a game against Drysdale that he would hit me before the night was over. There was some kind of tradition that Don would hit rookies. Now, I felt a relationship with Don. Same high school, and after my first hit in 1965, he did come by and congratulate me at my celebration with my family and friends. Walking up to the plate and seeing this giant of a man with the most menacing look on his face was not comforting. Second pitch, into the rib cage. You try not to show any pain as you stumble down to first base. I looked over at Morgan in the dugout and he tipped his hat. Thanks for the warning, Joe, it certainly eases the pain. I guess that was another one of those welcomes to the big leagues. Fucking traditions are starting to kill me.

There were some crazy moments, too. Just before starting a game against Pittsburgh, I was told by the skipper if I get a base hit to right field not to round the base. Just stand on it. My expression got me an explanation. That guy in right field, Clemente, will throw behind you if he thinks you made too big a turn. Roberto Clemente, my idol! So with that on my mind, I stepped up to the plate in the first inning. Bob Moose on the mound, a fastball, slider pitcher. I ripped a fastball to right field and as I approached first base I had amnesia, and made a turn towards second. Clemente scooped the ball up and it sure looked for a moment like he was going to throw to second. Then, as predicted, he wheeled towards first and threw a laser to Stargell. I was frozen in my tracks. Stargell caught the ball, took two steps towards me, smiled and tagged me out. You dumb shit, I thought. It's moments like this when the last place you want to go is to your dugout. Grady was not happy at all. "Fuck, you finally get a hit and you let that guy throw you out after I warned you. Horseshit rookies!" I grabbed my glove and just took a seat at the other end.

I was playing right field that night and as I took the field, Clemente ran by me and winked. That made everything okay. I took my position in right and looked down. I was standing in Roberto Clemente's footprints and that was overwhelming.

Grady Has No Sense Of Humor

I didn't exactly have a good relationship with the skipper. The team's playing poorly, I'm hitting terrible and he's miserable. In fact, he got to a point where at home games he had a chair in the tunnel just below the dugout where he would sit when things were bad. We were losing to the Mets one night, Grady was in the tunnel and Jerry Grote, the Mets catcher, kept fouling off pitches. Each time the crowd would get louder. After about eight foul balls, Grady wanted to know what the hell was going on up there. I was on the steps between Grady and the field. I said there are line drives everywhere; it looks like a track meet up here. He jumps out of his chair races up the steps and starts yelling for the bullpen to get ready. Then he notices no one is on base and Al Heist, a coach, tells him Grote has fouled off several pitches. If looks could kill, I'm pretty much buried.

As the season was coming to an end, I was notified that I would be going to basic training at Ft. Bliss in El Paso the day after the season ended in LA.

I managed to have one more encounter with Grady. Just before the LA trip, we got our asses whipped in a double header in Cincinnati. The clubhouse at Crosley Field was old and hot and so was the skipper. As I was putting on my black silk boxers he stopped by my locker and screamed. "The way you play, you don't belong in those damn fruitcake shorts." He was probably right, but I was into fashion. The next day I wore no underwear and got an even a worse look.

That final game came at Dodger Stadium on a Sunday afternoon. Bo Belinsky, the famous playboy ballplayer, who was at the end of his career with us, was going to throw me a going away party. I was leaving for Ft. Bliss at midnight. The game was quick, as most last games are when your team is out of the race. "Swing at the first pitch" is kind of the mantra of the day.

After the game, I told my Mom and Dad good-bye and it was off to the party. They didn't know all the facts, but wished me well.

A beautiful home in Hollywood, with beautiful women everywhere and me. Oh, there were other people there, I guess, but I was having the time of my life. You just wish you could store it up like a squirrel gathering nuts. Thank you, thank you, Bo Belinsky.

The Mod Look – it worked in the late 60s

I Could Really Throw A Hand Grenade

It was just hours later when I was having my head shaved, being yelled at and certainly not being issued silk boxers. Welcome to Ft. Bliss for the winter.

It was Vietnam time, and I had just come from Dodger Stadium still smelling like Hollywood, and these crazy people were yelling and screaming at me and the others. Tough adjustment. Then my first day as a recruit I got in a fight. That night the commanding officer ordered me into his office. I knocked on the door. "There's a woodpecker at my door."

What the hell does that mean? I went in. "Drop and give me 25 pushups." Well, I was in great shape obviously, so I gave him a few more. What do I know about the Army?

"You a ballplayer?" I can't believe it, I have a fan.

"Yes sir."

"What kind?"

"Baseball."

"I hate baseball."

"Well, I'm sorry to hear that." I was thinking, where's all this going?

"I understand you got in a fight today."

"Yes sir."

"I like that."

"I'm glad sir."

"Give me 25 more and get back to your barracks."

I had no idea what to make of that, but it wouldn't take long. I guess I was considered a privileged person, so things were going to get a little tough for me.

I started hearing things like, "You'll quit when Miller quits." And special assignments were given to me. Like, "You're the enemy, sneak over there and steal their weapons. If you get caught, too bad." I was not making friends and something had to change. I realized that with a few bucks I could get some drill sergeants to talk to the CO and ease up. Maybe an occasional bottle of Cutty Sark on Fridays would help. Whatever it took. I was tired of being the example every day and tired of defending myself in the barracks. I had to live by my wits.

Also, I could throw a hand grenade - the CO like that. And at the 40-yard low crawl, I was the fastest. So now he had me competing against other companies. I was his little toy. Things got easier from that point.

I graduated Soldier of the Cycle and stood on the bandstand as the troops marched by, giving me the finger. Who cares? It's over and after a couple of months at Fort Huachuca in Arizona, I would be out and heading towards spring training.

Would This Calm Me Down?

Just before leaving for the '68 season, I made a big move. I got engaged. High school sweetheart, Vicki Polito, said yes. It shocked everyone. But while those in shock were asking, I left for spring training.

As always, there were a lot of new faces. It was hard to believe I was entering my fifth year in professional baseball at just 22. I dreamed of coming to camp some year where I was penciled in from the beginning as the starting right fielder. I read all the articles in magazines and newspapers and "prospect" was still attached to my name. But it's a constant fight for a position. You're paid by the year, one year at a time. I was now at $9,000 per season, a $1,500 raise, and I had to fight like hell to get that.

So, here we go again, the clubhouse meetings, the fundamentals, the Grapefruit League and bus trips. This shit gets older, quicker, each year. The ball club kept the pressure on to win every game in the spring. We were worn out by the last week. It didn't make sense, the moment we leave camp, it's all forgotten anyway.

It was time for some turnover in the lineup. Doug Rader was, as he had promised, the starting third baseman, and quickly becoming popular as the "Red Rooster." Jesus Alou had joined us, one of the three Alou brothers in the bigs. Curt Blefary came over from Baltimore with some credentials. Change is constant, looking for the right combination.

We broke camp and I was the starting right fielder. I got off to a pretty good start. It takes time to adjust to the big leagues for most. It's so god damn hard, the pressure to perform is always there. I continued my Army meetings and then found myself back in Oklahoma, again, for a while. I got my stroke back and was called up, and this time I hoped it would be for good.

Grady Hatton was put out of his misery and fired by Spec Richardson, the GM. Our new manager was Harry "The Hat" Walker, who came from Pittsburgh Pirates. He was known as a hitting guru.

Pop And Glide

(or how to fuck up a team)

S o, now I'm in my fifth year and even though the game stays the same, I'm always playing for someone with different ideas. It's kind of like having a new boss at work every year.

So Harry "The Hat" Walker enters the locker room. He called a meeting and didn't shut up for an hour. From Leeds, Alabama, he just ranted and raved about what we had to do. What we really had to do was get dressed and get out on the field. He just got fired from the Pirates and now here he is with us. Goofy looking, too.

Harry loved to hang around the batting cage. Talking and talking. Nobody really ever taught me how to hit, I could just hit. And that's how everybody in the big leagues feels. That's how they got there. But Harry had a theory. And to make it more interesting, he thought everybody should hit the same. He called it "pop 'n' glide." We really thought he was kidding. Then he suggested we all use the same bat, a U1. The U1 kind of had a bottle shape, with no knob on the end.

Most of the veterans took a token swing with Harry's bat and then threw it away. The younger guys, he just preyed on. I'm fighting to stay in the big leagues, so I tried poppin 'n' glidin. Basically it's hitting off your front foot and adjusting as the pitch comes in. He loved it when you hit the ball to the opposite field.

Harry's theory was, the longer you waited on the pitch the better you saw it. Well, that wasn't anything new, but hitting off your front foot was. Some could do it, but it wasn't natural for most, including me, and it wouldn't work if it isn't natural. So making this drastic change in the big leagues pissed a lot of guys off.

It seems at Pittsburgh, Matty Alou had won the batting title playing for Harry and Harry was taking the credit for Alou's success. A bona fide fucking hitting genius. So we popped and glided into our slumps.

John Mayberry was a first round draft pick out of Detroit. A very large man who could hit the ball out of Yellowstone Park. Harry thought he would be more consistent poppin and glidin. Can you imagine? You look for years for a big power-hitting first baseman and then you turn him into a "Punch and Judy" hitter? This was going to be a long year for the 'Stros.

It became relentless. Harry had pictures of hitters in an album, and he was always walking around the locker room showing them. Guys would hide in the shower, the shitter wherever they could hide to get away.

During the game, you would be up at the plate and hear a whistle from Harry. You'd reluctantly look back in the dugout, and he's telling you to go the other way with the ball. I got so frustrated after grounding out to short for about the 20th time in a week, I came in the dugout and told Harry I'm through "poppin 'n' glidin." I'm going to my "leap and sweep." Where I went was the bench for a while.

The good news was, we had some new coaches and one of them was Mel McGaha, my former manager at Oklahoma City. He was the outfield coach, so I could talk to him. Coaches really have little authority in baseball, but you can talk to them. The reality is, coaches in the big leagues are just trying to make a living and get some pension time.

Whenever we played the Pirates, guys would always ask us around the cage how we liked Harry. No answer was necessary; the expressions on our faces were enough.

Driving Harry Nuts

It was fun to watch Harry on the bench when Rader hit. Doug drove Harry crazy from day one. I remember a day in San Francisco when Doug struck out three straight times against Juan Marichal. You had to watch Doug closely when he was having a bad day. He is the strongest and most unpredictable human being I've ever seen. He could and would tear toilets from walls, pop lights, break benches in half and, on special days, hit himself in the forehead 'til he had welts. When he returned to the bench after the third strikeout, he sat next to Harry. There was silence from the players. This could get bizarre. Harry was dying to say something to Doug. Doug just turned to Harry and said, "I've got him figured out now. Next time up, you know what I'm going to do Harry? Strike out again!"

Doug Rader was truly a character of unmatched stature. Also a young guy that played this game as hard as it could be played. Big, strong, no pain threshold and fear of nothing. Also very intelligent, but an attention span on the short side.

We had an off night in Pittsburgh and a few of us decided to go see a movie. Now that in itself was rare. One of those old grand theaters in downtown Pittsburgh.

We rarely sat together, so I took a seat and noticed Doug two rows directly behind me. As the curtain went up I turned and noticed he was the only one in his row. People were trying to sit in his row, but they were being told by Doug the entire row was saved. Something about Doug scares people because they all moved on. Suddenly there was the sound of somebody getting slapped on the head. It was right behind me. I looked back and Doug had slapped a bald man on the head that was sitting between Doug and me, and ordered him to get my popcorn. I handed it to the poor soul and he handed it to Doug. Shortly after another slap, my popcorn came back. Doug just has a way of getting his way.

Not everything that happens on or off the field is funny. One of the worst, in fact, happened on a hot rainy afternoon game in St. Louis. Wade Blasingame was the starting pitcher. After a brief rain delay, we took the field. The hitter was Julian Javiar. Javiar hit a line drive up the middle that hit Blasingame right in the balls. I've never heard a sound like that. It sounded like someone hitting a concrete wall with a bat. "Blazer" went down immediately and we rushed to the mound. He was out cold, but his body was lurching up and down. The trainer screamed to get him in the clubhouse. We picked him up and rushed up the tunnel and into the training room. The Card's doctor rushed in. The sounds coming out of Blasingame were frightening. The doctor screamed, "Get an ambulance here." We all backed out of the way.

One testicle shattered. Out for almost two months, he called me when he was released from the hospital so I could pick him up at the airport. As he slowly got in my car, the first words out of his mouth were "I'm ready to get my nut off." Blazer, it turned out, didn't wear a cup when he pitched. I wouldn't take a team picture without a cup on.

Unfortunately, I don't think Wade was ever the same. I don't know how you could be. Naturally, when we arrived at his locker upon return, he had cups of all sizes from his friendly and compassionate teammates.

Another great thing Harry brought to the Astros was curfew. Now this was not new. Every team at one time or another has curfews, but every fucking night on the road? When the bus got back to the hotel after a game, our curfew would be announced. Usually a couple of hours following the announcement. Their claim was that the only people out that late were whores and robbers. And us! Hell, it took us a couple of hours to have some cocktails and unwind. Besides, we sleep all day, so what's the point? Now, we all had to become sneaky little devils. You know, be in our rooms when the coach called and then maybe if it was worth it, out the door and down the stairs we would go. Come on, we're grown men - well maybe not quite - but curfew checks every night? Give me a break.

It became important to know certain bellman and which back doors are open. In fact, for me it became a big game because I wasn't coming in on time every night.

This was not a happy team. Bring back Grady, even.

How To Screw Up A Wedding

We were fast approaching the end of the season, and my wedding. I was talking to Vicki, and she reminded me to be careful - just two more weeks. So, there I was in right field, the bases were loaded. A long fly was hit over my head. I broke back and as the ball hit my glove, I ran right into the right field wall at the Astrodome. They say it was the loudest collision they ever heard. As I laid there in agony, looking up, the fans were screaming down at me to get up and throw the ball in. I didn't get up; it was an inside-the-park home run with the bases loaded.

The trainer, Jim Ewell, knelt down beside me. Some of my teammates surrounded me. My roommate, Wade, said "Nice catch, dummy". I looked at the trainer. "Alright, tell me what hurts."

"I have a brain concussion and my knee is killing me." He then asked how my left ankle felt. I raised my spinning head and oh, my god! My right ankle was going north and south, my left, east and west. Poor Vicki, she's going to freak out.

I was carried off the field and taken to Methodist Hospital emergency room, where it was quickly determined: a major break in the ankle. As I was sitting on a table, half undressed with my uniform top on, someone pulled back the drapes around me. A Dr. DeBakey peeked in. I recognized him from the news; something to do with heart transplants. I was not dying, I informed him, and he was gone.

Once they got me settled with a cast and in my room, I made that call to the bride. Guess what? Vicki was clueless, "You got a home run?"

"No not quite. But I did break my ankle." There was silence.

The wedding was just two weeks away and the honeymoon was planned. Dr. Brelsford, the team doctor, didn't want me gone long. So the honeymoon was cut short. I asked if I could have a walking cast and he just laughed and put more and more plaster on.

My wife-to-be, after the shock, surprised me the morning of our wedding with crutches beautifully decorated in ivy and flowers. Hated it, but what the hell could I do about it?

A brief couple of days in Las Vegas and then it was back to Houston to set up our new home and be where the doctor could watch my progress.

Vicki knows I will do anything for attention

A Raise Is A Good Thing

By the time spring rolled around, I was ready. A slight limp, but I was really ready to get to Florida. I knew this was going to be my chance to be the starting right fielder. I had gotten my new contract and I had gotten a $3,000 raise. I'm getting up there, now, $12,000 a year. With that kind of pay, they must be really counting on me. Another thing that helped was my mom and dad were paying our apartment rent, since I couldn't work in the off season.

The first day of spring brought something new to the game. Spec and Harry had brought the "Exer-Genie" to camp. I can only explain it as a series of dynamic tension exercises with this strange little tube with a rope in it. Every day, before we actually played the game of baseball, we were put through agony. More guys were hurting than ever, and bitching and moaning took on a whole new meaning.

If that wasn't enough, after each practice or game we had to run the Astro mile. This was really dumb. As I'm dragging my ass doing the mile, Harry starts yelling. "You better get going."

"Shit, Harry, I'm a goddamn sprinter, not a distance runner." Everybody laughed but Harry. By the end of camp, we had sabotaged most of the Exer-Genie machines and they finally realized the last week, we were all exhausted.

Baseball people are always looking for the extra thing. How about more batting practice and fielding, wouldn't that be unusual, we thought.

Practice What?

I was the opening day right fielder and nobody was going to get me out of there. This felt like the best team we'd had in years. All-star catcher, John Edwards, Rader, Metzger, Morgan, Pepitone, Wynn, Watson and of course, yours truly. We had good pitching led by Larry Dierker and a young phenom and former Little League friend of mine, Tom Griffin.

There was a fly ball down the right field line curving foul. I always had a mind- set to catch everything. Boom, right into the stands I ran. This was my first attempt of the season and the first since I'd run into the wall the year before and broke my ankle. I went down; déjà vu, I guess. This time no breaks, just bruises but I stayed in the game.

The next day, sore but naturally not going to admit it or go near the training room. Mel McGaha came by my locker. "How do you feel?"

"Good. Get dressed, Harry wants me to take you downstairs and teach you how to run into walls."

I laughed, "That's funny, Mel."

"I'm serious, get dressed."

You have got to be shitting me. Mel and Salty Parker were waiting. Salty started to hit balls over my head and Mel said to feel the warning track, know how much room you have. I hated this. First of all, I'm a balls-out player. second of all, I think this is a Harry Conspiracy to get me hurt for good. Practice running into walls?. Why don't you just release me or trade me? Poor Mel, just doing his job. Okay, so I came up short of the wall, showed that I understood and that was that. Stupid fucking manager.

Playing every day was fun. When you know you're in the lineup, you can actually rest during the day. You don't sit around wondering. You come to the park excited. Also, seeing pitching every day makes it so much easier to hit. I got hot and stayed hot.

As you go to the different cities, fans start to take notice. Some are friendly, and then there's New York. I started my first game in Shea against Tom Seaver. First time up, I struck out. As I returned to the outfield, the fans were all over me. Next time same results at the plate, the fans even louder. After my third strike out against Seaver, the entire outfield stands were eating me alive. "You're pathetic, go back to the bushes, you couldn't hit me if I ran across home plate." You hear all this. And as it gets louder, your ass tightens up more. I knew I had one more shot at Seaver. I came through with a single. As I returned to the outfield with my head up, I shot them the finger. They loved it. They loved the fact I acknowledged them. Fans for life.

How fun was this? Driving in runs, getting interviewed after the game, I'm a starting right fielder in the big leagues. The countless hours of dreaming. The thousands of swings I took as a kid in front of the mirror announcing my own at-bat. Now I can't get enough of hearing "Now hitting, number 21, right fielder, Norm Miller."

Those guys were crazy. I think the game makes you that way. You play every day for months. The pressure, travel, bizarre eating habits, late nights of fun.

I remember returning from a two-week road trip. I laughed my ass off that early morning as the bus pulled up to the Astrodome. All the wives and kids waiting. It's about 2:30 AM and Blasingame grabs the microphone and says, "Alright all you guys, try and act horny."

Not everybody fooled around. Those who didn't, wished they did, however. There were some days, especially in Chicago, with all day games, guys would get in that old wood-floor locker room and look like shit. You've got a couple of hours and you're going to be facing 95 mile-an-hour fastballs. Somehow, these guys could do it. A pot of coffee and a "greenie" and off we went.

A greenie, for those that don't know, was a small amphetamine. With a little coffee, it woke you up. It certainly didn't turn you into Babe Ruth or help you throw a no-hitter.

Personally I had some of my most "horseshit games" when I was exhausted for whatever reason, and took a greenie. It was no big deal back then, because really it was psychological.

Chicago was always fun. Wrigley field and Rush Street. Can't get any better than that. Play the game, hit the bars. Finely-tuned athletes, we were. Most drank a lot, smoked cigarettes, hell it was the 60's.

In '68, during the Democratic convention, we were in town and staying in the Chicago Hilton - convention headquarters. Other than the riots outside, other than armed militia everywhere in the hotel, it was just another day at the ballpark for us. We're fucking ballplayers, that's it.

The weeks and months just kept going good. I was batting right around .300 all year, lots of key hits, playing right field well. An article in Sport Magazine came out where I was considered one of the ten most underrated players in the National League. I was doing everything I could to be a fixture in the lineup. The clubhouse was loose and nuts. You'd walk in and Rader would be practicing his slap shots with a hockey puck. The guys were loose and ripping each other to pieces. I remember making an error one night that cost us the game. Imagine how bad you feel when you do something like that. I was shaving after the game. Fred Gladding came in and took the blade out of the razor and handed to me. "Here shave with this; maybe you'll cut your throat". You can't blame Fred, he was on the mound when I fucked up the play. It was all in good humor. Hell, I was just happy to be part of all this. Besides tomorrow is another day and I just might hit one out to win the game. That's the beauty of baseball, tomorrow is another day.

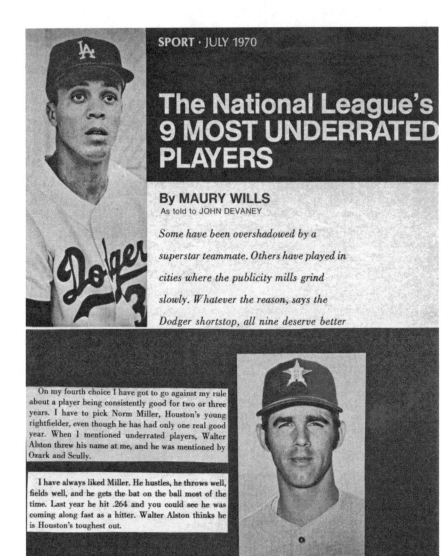

The National League's 9 MOST UNDERRATED PLAYERS

By MAURY WILLS
As told to JOHN DEVANEY

Some have been overshadowed by a superstar teammate. Others have played in cities where the publicity mills grind slowly. Whatever the reason, says the Dodger shortstop, all nine deserve better

On my fourth choice I have got to go against my rule about a player being consistently good for two or three years. I have to pick Norm Miller, Houston's young rightfielder, even though he has had only one real good year. When I mentioned underrated players, Walter Alston threw his name at me, and he was mentioned by Ozark and Scully.

I have always liked Miller. He hustles, he throws well, fields well, and he gets the bat on the ball most of the time. Last year he hit .264 and you could see he was coming along fast as a hitter. Walter Alston thinks he is Houston's toughest out.

Maury Wills, excellent judge of talent

The Shit Hits The Fan

The team was in San Diego for a weekend series. Saturday, I was not in the lineup. Nobody said why. They had a left-hander pitching, but I'd been playing every day. We hadn't platooned up until then, so why start? I had always hit left-handed pitching well, and we really didn't have a strong right-handed hitter on the bench.

A few of the players questioned me, but honestly, I just let it slide, figuring it's just a day off.

Sunday, another left-hander was pitching, and once again I'm not in there and still nothing was said to me. I guess I should ask someone, but I was trying to not rock the boat, the team has been going well. The players were really on me now. "Hey, sweetheart, you taking a weekend off? What's wrong, she has her period today?" I started to get pissed off. Two days on the bench rarely happens. What the hell is going on?

We flew on to Pittsburgh that night. On Monday night, the Pirates had a right- hander going and again, I was not in there. I was so pissed off by now. I asked the coaches, but they didn't know shit or won't tell me. I decided to go sit down in the bullpen as far away from Harry as I could. It was a close ballgame and as we approached the ninth inning, I knew the pitcher would be leading off and we would pinch hit. I started loosening up and then went to the dugout. I got my helmet and bat and when the top of the ninth came and the pitcher was due to lead off, I just took it upon myself to go to the on-deck circle. As the catcher threw the ball to second, Walker yelled at me to get back in the dugout. He was sending Keith Lampard, a rookie, up to hit. I slammed my bat down and threw my helmet at Harry and let him have it.

Nothing improved for two more days and by now it was becoming a story. I started to pop off to the press. On the last night after the game, I got shit-faced. We had an early flight to Chicago and I barely got back from the bar to pack and get on the bus. I threw my bags at the bus and walked up to Harry. "Why aren't I playing?"

"None of your goddamn business, now got your ass on the bus." From the Hilton to the Airport I was all over him. The press rides the bus and they were writing away. My teammates in the back of the bus were doing everything to encourage me to keep it up. I was relentless.

That evening, Spec Richardson, our GM, called me from Houston to tell me he was not happy about my actions. "Well, fuck you and Harry both," was my response. "I've played every game, driving in runs, doing a great job and I'm supposed to just sit down and keep quiet? No fucking way. I want out of here." Spec said he's coming to Chicago and we will meet in the morning, and hung up.

I took a cab to the ballpark instead of the team bus. I was not talking to anyone. I still wasn't in the lineup. I put on my uniform and went down for batting practice. Harry and Spec were waiting for me on the bench. Harry had a Houston newspaper in his hand. When he saw me, he stood up and starting waving the paper at me. "You ungrateful son of a bitch. I'm the reason you're even here and you take shots at me in the paper like this."

"Harry, bite me. I earned that job and then you just take me out of the lineup and don't have the balls to tell me why and then tell me it's none of my goddamn business."

Spec tells me to sit down and shut up. "Shut up, my ass." Walker grabs me and we start to wrestle. I wanted to kill him. I didn't know what to do next. I went back up in the locker room and just sat at my locker trying to calm me down. The players came back up from batting practice. Tom Griffin came by, "Hey, 'stormin,' you're in there today, calm down and stick it up their ass." Salty Parker came by and showed me the new lineup, back in the third spot. I had to do everything I could to calm down and try and get my head straight.

I managed to get a couple of hits, but from that point to the end of the season, my playing time was not the same.

Now I'm young, high-strung and tenacious. But I had made up my mind that Harry and I were never going to work. My game suffered the rest of the year, my batting average dropping to .264. If I play every day I can hit; if I don't I'm just not as good.

You only have a few years to make it. If you're lucky. The average life of a major leaguer is about four and a half years. I knew I could play and I knew it had to be somewhere else.

I Want Out Of Here

I wasted no time. The day the season ended, I got up and went to Spec Richardson's office. I walked right past Ann Wallace, his secretary, and into his office. He was on the phone, feet on the credenza, cigar in mouth. He turned around and told me to sit down. He ended his conversation and asked what I wanted. I said, "Out of here." "You know, Norm, there're probably five teams I could trade you to today, but you know what, it isn't going to happen. So I suggest you get your ass out of here now."

You have absolutely no control over your career. What was I going to do? The man just told me other teams want me. I'm young, I can hit, but I play for a manager that I can't stand and a GM who just wants to control my life. This was going to be a long winter.

When I arrived at spring training, I decided to put everything behind me. I had gotten a raise to $15,000 without even fighting for it. There was very little talk. Hell, I wouldn't even look at Harry. But I hustled and decided to just do what I do. Other teams are always watching. Opening day, I was in the starting lineup. For the second time in three years, I hit a home run on opening day. Things went well in June. My average was good and fun was back in my game. Then it was time for my annual two weeks of Army summer camp.

A New Guy Appears And He's ... Good

Upon my return, I noticed a new person in the clubhouse, Cesar Cedeno, young prospect we had heard a lot about. Knowing he was an outfielder I kept a close eye on him. That first time we took pre-game infield together I noticed his arm was more like a cannon. He was built like Adonis and could run like the wind. He would make a perfect center fielder, except we already had Jimmy Wynn, the "Toy Cannon," out there. Since I was coming off two weeks of inactivity, Cesar got his start. Sitting on the bench that night, I realized oh, shit. You always hear there's always someone that can take your job, and as much as I hated to admit it, this guy looked great.

From June on, there wasn't much I could do. I couldn't get pissed because the players would make my life miserable. It's all about winning and the team, and if this guy is helping out, you've got to pull for him. So my role was quickly changing. My mind-set had to adjust.

Now, I knew I'm only 24, teams know me, so I have to do what I can do to get noticed and maybe, just maybe, Cedeno's arrival will get me out of Houston and back in a lineup somewhere else.

When the press talked to me, I was upbeat. In the locker room, I agitated others and fucked around as much as I could. When I got the chance to play, I hustled. Believe me, the one thing I didn't want to do is piss off my teammates.

I was doing a lot of pinch-hitting in pressure situations. I decided to start calling myself the "secret weapon." As the games would get in a position that I might be called upon, I would start to roam the dugout, getting myself worked-up into a frenzy. I would wear my jacket like a cape. Rage would build. The guys on the bench would tell me to get the hell out of their way. I didn't care; I was the "secret weapon." This act got me motivated, and with that came success. I did the job more times than not. The press picked up on this and so did the fans. And it was fun, certainly better than being pissed off all the time.

But I wanted out, I wanted to play.

Two Jobs

I always worked in the off-season because even though $15,000 was
good money. It wasn't enough to live the lifestyle a major leaguer
wanted to live. Besides, my folks were no longer paying our rent.

My first job in Houston was manager of the men's department
at Battlesteins Department store. You know, walk around, mingle with
the people and approve checks.

I met a fan that was in the investment business who let me hang
around with him a little. It was interesting, learning about business. A
little of this, a little of that. He suggested I get my real estate license; it
might pay off in the future. So I studied and got it.

In 1971 the Astros made a huge trade, sending Joe Morgan,
Jack Billingham and Denis Menke to the Reds for Tommy Helms, Lee
May and Jimmy Stewart. This was big. Unfortunately it did nothing for
me. So it was off to Cocoa once again as the fourth outfielder and
secret weapon. Once again I got a pay raise without asking and I was
up to $20,000. I stayed on Spec to trade me and I kept hearing the same

thing. "If you don't like it here, quit." That's how the game treated you, besides where could I go? They owned me for life.

We hadn't finished higher than fourth since Harry showed up. At some point, I kept thinking, one of us would be gone.

Larry Dierker had written an Astros Fight Song. Harry had no respect at this point and we sang it to Harry whenever we could. Larry had written a verse for just about every player, but the chorus was what made it. "When we win our game each day, then what the fuck can Harry say, it makes a fellow proud to be, as a kid I vowed to be, a no good fucking rowdy ASTRO!"

When we would get on the bus or airplane, Harry would put on his large earphones that were attached to nothing, just so he didn't have to hear our tribute to him.

We had tried to get Rader to kill him. One game, Harry and Doug went at it down in the tunnel. Yelling and screaming at each other. Only one returned. The coaches had to get Harry off a hook Doug had hung him on.

Once again, I was the caped crusader, coming to bat late in the game. I even painted lightning bolts on my shoes. That didn't go over well and the clubhouse boy was asked to paint over my creation. I did anything to keep my sanity. The years were clicking off. I knew I could start for many teams, but here I was wasting away on the bench.

My season was cut short in '71. I was facing Bill Singer of the Dodgers. I hit a fastball right up the middle off his shins. The ball ricochets to Richie Allen halfway between home and first base. Richie scooped it up and I had three choices. Stop and let him tag me, try and go around him or go through him. I chose through him. I went down hard and the result was I was out at first and out with a broken wrist. Bad move. Why do I keep running into things?

Image Problem?

I think my injury played right into the hands of the ball club. Over the past couple of years, there had been published reports that other teams wanted me. The Astros never had a response. Often the local press would ask Spec or Harry why I wasn't utilized more. "Injury-prone, the guy gets hurt." Injury-prone is something you don't want hung around your neck. I got hurt twice in collisions hustling. Injury-prone meant chronic injuries like ankle sprains, hamstrings, those types of injuries. I'm a gamer. I was really pissed when "injury-prone" came out.

My career was status quo. I was in the big leagues but not going anywhere. We were a .500 team going nowhere. Baseball is full of rumors. Players love to sit around making up trades and then there is always the talk of when the manager was getting the axe.

As a team, nobody liked Harry. One of the things that continued to kill us was his constant hammering at guys. Hell, he lost all the respect of the players. Also, he was the type of manager that second-guessed everything you did. "Why did you swing at that pitch? Why did you throw him a curveball?" That gets real old.

One of the things he used to always say when we had a double play situation was "Let's get one for sure, now." I hate that. Guys would jump up and yell, "Fuck one; let's get two."

At this point, baseball was only fun before and after the game. But we kept singing Harry his song. The press was finally putting pressure on that genius, General Manager, Spec Richardson.

I was mainly pinch-hitting and so frustrated. The longer you sit on the bench, the less chance other teams will want you. I felt like I might spend my entire career in oblivion. I used to be a prospect and somehow I had become a suspect.

Pittsburgh Can Be Dangerous

E ven my life off the field got crazy. One night, several of us were in a joint in downtown Pittsburgh. Kind of an all-night dive. We liked those places. The bartenders were good to us, and there was very little riff raff hanging around us. It was early in the morning, around 2 AM. I was sitting in a booth just having my scotch and talking innocently to a couple of ladies. Rader, Menke, Edwards and Metzger were in the back room playing shuffle-board, having fun. Don Wilson walked in. He had been the starting pitcher that night and no one likes to be around Don when he pitches, win or lose. He approached me and the ladies and just sat down in the booth with us. Don had thrown a couple of no-hitters already in his career. On his good days, Don was predictable. On his pitching days, a loose cannon.

He always wore this black top-coat. I accidentally knocked over my drink and it spilled in his lap. He went off, telling me I didn't want a black guy sitting with white women. "Oh shit, here we go." It's the strange Don. The girls couldn't get out unless they climbed over us, and he just kept after me. It didn't take long and I just got up and took a seat at the bar. The girls bolted from the joint.

As I ordered another drink at the bar, Don kept up his rant. "You fucking Jew, you." I'd finally had enough and told him to just shut the fuck up. Suddenly, I was hit in my left ear and I remember flying off the bar stool, landing face down on the sawdust floor. He jumped on my back and put a strangle hold on me. From the back room, I could hear, "Kill the Jew, kill the Jew." Finally someone knocked Don off me when they realized that's exactly what he was doing. I crawled out the door on my hands and knees, and there I lay on the sidewalk, just trying to catch my breath. I made it back to the hotel, with curfew the least of my worries.

I tried to sleep but my neck was killing me and I had a nice ringing noise in my head. What to do about this? Early in the morning I got out the phone book and called a doctor for an appointment. This wasn't something I wanted the trainer to know about. I found one close by. As the elevator door opened, there stood all 6'4" of Don Wilson. "How you doing, Stormin?"

I grunted a barely audible, "Just great Don, quite frankly I never felt better." He had no clue that he had committed a felony on my body. I hopped in a cab and headed to the doctor. Nothing smashed or long-term, the doctor said, but I should get therapy on my neck. I told our trainer that I slept funny and I needed some therapy. Sitting in the trainer's room that night, Menke walked in and says, "What the hell's wrong with you?" I wanted to jump off the table and kill him for not backing me up. He smiled and left. I love these guys.

Now, let me say this, there was absolutely no prejudice ever with Don on that team until that night. As far as "kill the Jew," that's just my teammates being humorous. After all, there aren't many of us in the game, so that's that. None of it was personal. Ballplayers are not a politically correct group.

A New Manager And The Irony Of All Ironies

Finally, Harry "The Hat" Walker was fired. Who was going to be the next manager? Speculation was high. Somebody new? Somebody from the organization? Days went by and then it was announced. Hold on to your hats, ladies and gentlemen. With all the talent out there, Spec had outdone himself again. Another retread. This guy should be in cold storage. The one and only, Leo Durocher. My god, he ran the Cubs into the ground for years. We couldn't believe it? The news couldn't be worse. Leo Durocher, the guy who had said almost 20 years ago on national television that someday I would be in the big leagues, was now my manager. How ironic was this?

The night he showed up in that locker room was the beginning of a dark, dark time. After years with one old shit-head and now we got a relic. He walked in in all his splendor. Nobody greeted him. He was brought in for one reason. Sell tickets. And that's how he managed for 31 games. This wasn't his team, so he just took it easy and tried to be buddies with all of us. We had heard all about what it's like to play for this guy from Cub players.

So there he was telling Frank Sinatra stories to which nobody listened. Showing us his custom-made fag boots, which nobody liked, and name-dropping all the famous people that are his friends. He wore so much cologne the clubhouse started to smell like a whore house. So another .500 season came to an end. I continued as a bench player and pinch hitter. The winter months started to get more serious for me. Back in high school, when I was working out in the summer months with the Angels, Bob Rodgers, the catcher at that time and later a major-league manager, told me "Son, learn another profession because this game can spit you out real fast."

I continued learning the real estate business in Houston and started to meet good people. Bob Rodgers' advice was echoing in my ears.

How To Get On Leo's Shit List

Now, it was back to Cocoa and Leo's turn to make the Astros a winner. I was given the job of player representative. That is a thankless job and usually results in nothing good for the player that takes it. Kind of like a curse.

We were scheduled to play a spring training game in Pompano Beach. Marvin Miller, the head of the players' association, was going to meet with us and give us the annual "state of the union" speech. Leo decided to leave all the regulars back in camp. This raised a lot of eyebrows. The press was all over it. Marvin was great for the players, but management obviously didn't like him. I was on the bus with all the rookies and even some minor leaguers they sent for the trip. We met in the outfield after arriving in Pompano. In the middle of Marvin's meeting, here came Durocher out to the group. He told the players the meeting was over and had some words for Marvin. We were pissed. But without any of the regulars, we had no power. The meeting reluctantly broke up.

After returning to Cocoa that night, there was a press conference called. I was told to be there. The press was all over Leo for what he did. He tried to defend himself. I sat there listening to this fool. Then I was asked the point of view of the players. I said it was wrong and he had no right to leave the regulars at home and it was a classless act walking out on the field "like Napoleon."

The next morning as I walked out of the clubhouse and glanced at the lineup card for the game, I saw I wasn't in the lineup. Then, I noticed my name wasn't even listed as an extra. Then, I looked at the other daily assignments and there was no Norm Miller to be found. I figured just a mistake and walked out. The next day the same thing. When I started to ask a couple of coaches, they just skirted the issue, "Hey, I don't make out those things."

Teammates started asking, "Hey, Norm, what field you on today, number 12? Hey, Norm, you going fishing today?" As the bus rolled away for a road trip, they all waved good-bye. This was unbelievable. I was like a forgotten soul. So, I just wandered around, watching the minor leaguers. Sometimes I would jump in the cage and hit some balls. The writing was certainly on wall. In my entire career I had never seen anybody left off the daily list. I started looking around for Leo's shit list, because I had to be at the top of it. My days were numbered.

To everyone's surprise, I ended up breaking camp with the club. Sometimes trades take time. Every day, there would be notes in my locker. I'd open them up and they would say "Miller goes to Montreal for two ball boys and an usher." Or "Astros send Miller to Japan for two tons of rice." Don't laugh, I'm worth it.

The guys never let up. "Hey, Norm, be sure and ask for the player rep job wherever you end up, it worked well for you here." I know it sounds tough, but that's the game. Ballplayers are the greatest. If you can't take it, you won't get it. So in a bizarre way, that's their way of letting you know they care.

We opened the season in LA for a short, two-game series. That was a strange time in my life. I had been in Houston for a long time. It was my home now. But it had been a brutal week not knowing what was next.

My dad came down for breakfast and to see some of the guys. Over the years, he had met a lot of the players and everybody really liked him. Throughout my career, he never showed disappointment that I wasn't a star. He never questioned why I wasn't in the lineup more. He just loved coming to the ballpark. Whether I did good or bad, it was always about the game, not me. He wanted a ballplayer for a son, he had one and that was good enough.

I walk out of the Biltmore Hotel in downtown LA to catch an early cab to Dodger Stadium. I called home about every few hours to tell Vicki, "Nothing yet." I didn't even unpack my suitcase, knowing that it could be any moment my life would change along with my address.

I've Been Shot – No, Traded

Tommy Helms and Jimmy Stewart are out front. A cab pulls up, they hop in ahead of me. As I put one foot into the cab, suddenly I felt a pain in my lower left side that knocked me down like I had been shot. I lay in agony. Helms and Stewart didn't know what to think. I guess they thought I had slipped. "I've been shot," I remember screaming. The cabbie came around. They loaded me like a sack of potatoes in the cab and took me to the ballpark, which is only minutes from downtown. I was lying in the back seat when we got to Dodger Stadium, Helms and Stewart got out and left me. The cabbie didn't know what the fuck to do. A few minutes later, the trainer arrived with a cart. They wheeled me into the locker room and slid me on the training table. I was quickly reassured I hadn't been shot. Jim Ewell, the trainer, was on the phone with a doctor. Then Durocher came in. "What the fuck happened to him?" If I could have gotten up, I would have decked him. Jim Ewell just said, "We don't know yet." Leo just turned and walked out. What an asshole.

It felt like hours, but in a few minutes the Dodger doctor, Dr. Kerlan, came in. He grabbed my big toe and told me to hold it up as he bent down. So, I have a limp toe, what does that mean? He continued to examine me. Then, he suggested to Jim Ewell that they get me back to Houston as soon as possible. It didn't sound good and it felt worse.

By now the entire team had arrived and came in the training room with some compassionate thoughts. "Nobody gets hurt getting into a damn cab. What a shame, you were back in the lineup tonight." Liars.

Hours later, Art Perkins the traveling secretary, called me and said they had me on a flight that evening back to Houston. I was just doped up, scared and ready to go home. I must have called Vicki, because she was there when I came off the plane in a wheelchair.

The next morning, it was off to Dr. Brelsford's office. Severe muscle strain and spasms. We'll put you in the hospital for a few days, knock you out and let things cool down. I didn't buy it. I love you Dr. B. but this wasn't just spasms. I've had those and this was worse. I convinced him to let me go home and dope me up.

It was Saturday, five days since this had all started. I hadn't moved for days, just zoned out. The phone rang and Vicki got it. She came in and said, "It's Spec and he wants to know if you feel strong enough to come to the game and sit with him." This made no sense to me, but I said I would be there.

I could barely walk, my left leg felt dead and I looked like shit. Vicki and I got to Spec's box on the press level just as the first pitch was thrown. Curiosity had replaced a lot of pain as I sat there inning after inning wondering why he got me out of bed.

The game ended. I shuffled back to our car and went home, absolutely nothing had changed. By now the pain had just about overwhelmed me. By the time we pulled into our garage, I just wanted to crawl into bed and take my pills. The phone rang as we walked in the house. It was 10:30 PM; Vicki reached for the phone. She handed it to me and just looked deep into my eyes.

I hung up the phone. "Where?" "Atlanta." Vicki, by the way, was almost nine months pregnant. We both just sat down at the kitchen table. Then the phone rang, again. I grabbed it. It was Eddie Robinson, the GM for the Braves. Then I heard another familiar voice, Eddie Mathews, the manager. They called to welcome me. Eddie Mathews was one of my boyhood idols and also a teammate in '67. Now he was going to be my manager. They were excited, but I told them, "Don't make this trade, I'm hurt." Robinson, who was actually the Farm Director for Houston back in '64 and drafted me from the Angels, said, "We know all about it. We actually made the trade on Monday. The doctors have all talked."

I said it again, "It's worse then they're saying." It all seemed to fall on deaf ears. They wanted me to take my time and join them Tuesday in Atlanta. Vicki and I didn't know what the fuck to do. She's huge and I'm useless.

Rolling Into Atlanta

When I landed in Atlanta and was wheeled off the plane in a wheelchair, the look on Eddie Robinson's face said it all. Within hours, I was admitted to Piedmont Hospital.

Some serious probing by Dr. Wells, the Braves' doctor, was waiting for me. It was surreal. Finally traded to a team that really wanted me and here I was, alone in a hospital. My other concern, obviously, was Vicki, at home alone. The Braves' front office was staying in touch, I even heard from the owner, Bill Bartholomay, assuring me they would take good care of me and my family.

Vicki decided that she was coming to Atlanta and our baby would be born there. The Braves took good care of us, making sure Vicki and her mom got there safely and were made comfortable.

I heard from a friend in Houston. Imagine this, the fellow they traded me for, Cecil Upshaw showed up with a sore arm. There were rumors in the paper that I might be coming back to Houston, the trade voided. I deserved better luck than all this. I lay there for days concerned about my future and becoming a dad.

Then the owner, Mr. Bartholomay, called. They wanted to send me to Elgin, Illinois, to see a Dr. Lyman Smith. It seems he had a new procedure and in discussions with the Braves doctors, thought I was a good candidate for it. I just wanted to do anything to get back in the game. "Sure, I'll go."

Elgin, Illinois, is not far from Chicago. I checked in and Dr. Smith came by. He had something called a Chymopapain Injection procedure. They were going to inject something derived from the Papaya fruit into the disc in my lower back. This magic would shrink the swelling of the disk and I would feel better. Kind of sounded like "witch doctor shit" to me, but at this point I'll give it a go.

I woke up after the procedure with a couple of Band-Aids on my side. I felt little or no pain for the first time in weeks. Two days later, I was on a plane heading back to Atlanta, but this time I went to the stadium, not the hospital. It was a miracle.

Bill Acree was the first to welcome me as I walked into the clubhouse. He used to be in charge of the visiting clubhouse, but now he was the "general" of the home-team clubhouse. He took me down to my locker, number 42 jersey hanging there. Right next to me was number 44 – Henry Aaron.

Eddie Mathews came in and seemed really pleased to see me. He sat down to chat. "We've been trying to get you for a long time," he said. "When you're ready, right field is yours." Finally, at 27 years old, I got another chance at playing every day. All I have to do is get back in shape and my career is getting a jump-start.

The first time I put on the Braves uniform was surreal. For years, I'd had an orange and blue shooting star across my chest. Now I had this blue and white softball-looking uniform. Everything seemed so different, but I was sure once I got back in the lineup, I would feel right at home.

Another first for me was meeting Hank Aaron. He came in, sat down and I couldn't believe my eyes. Here is one of the greatest, reaching out to shake my hand. This was worth all the pain the past few weeks. I tried not to stare at the legend. I had seen him play from the other dugout for years, but my god, he's bigger than I thought.

One by one, they came by to greet me. I was told to take my time; it had only been a few days since the pain was relieved by Dr. Smith. It was like starting over, and as bad as I wanted to play, it was a slow process. My legs were weak; I had lost a lot of weight. Dave Pursely, the Braves trainer, watched me closely.

That first start as a Brave finally came. It was so much fun to play again. I always had played well in Fulton County Stadium, so I was confident. It didn't take long, though, for my luck to change.

I slid into third base and couldn't get up. Everything in my back tightened up and I had to be helped off the field. As I lay on the training table, the doctors were on the phone. One of the side effects of the procedure I had in Elgin was severe muscle spasms and I was experiencing that right then. That was it.

I reentered Piedmont for some more tests and daily therapy. The spasms were rough. Then my wife decided it was time, so she checked in. Alyson was born, and both of us were patients. How ironic, I'm a father for the first time - something new - but I'm out of the lineup after just a few innings - something old.

We both managed to get out of the hospital and move into an apartment with our baby daughter. I went to the ballpark every day for treatments. I walked and walked around the field but my year was over.

A Witness To History

I continued working hard all winter. Henry Aaron was going to break Babe Ruth's home run record and I was looking forward to being part of history.

We had a new manager in Atlanta, Clyde King, a long-time baseball man I knew nothing about. When I met him in spring training, he seemed very mild-mannered, easy-going. At this point of my career, my likes or dislikes for managers and general managers really didn't matter. Hell, trainers and doctors had become what mattered to me. But I was not going to give up. I had not lost my love of the game and I was still young - well, maybe my mind was, but my body certainly had had a rough couple of years.

Camp in West Palm Beach went well. They all take on their own personalities. Early in my career, the objective was to get noticed. Then it was fight for a position. Then we kind of moved into the maintain-your-role position. Now I was fighting to stay in the game, and I knew if my back could hold together I would still fulfill some of my dreams.

The Braves had some good players. Davey Johnson, Darrell Evans, Ralph Garr, Dusty Baker, but the attention was on one man. It was a lot of fun to watch how a legend went about his business. The career of Aaron had been understated and certainly not over-rated. His consistency to play the game year after year at the highest level is beyond reproach. And in a very short time, he was going to surpass one of the most, if not the most, coveted records in sports: Babe Ruth's career home run record of 714.

Lockering next to Hank the previous year was truly a highlight. To watch and listen to this man handle the same questions every day with class and style was a pleasure. To have the privilege of having lunch with Henry a couple of times, just he and I, was something I'll never forget. We also shared the same birthday. Well, lucky me. I'm sure it didn't mean shit to him.

He would stroll out to the plate like he did everything - smoothly. It looked effortless how he swung the bat, ran the bases or caught a fly ball on the run. The reporters and cameras were everywhere.

But these was not easy times for Hank. He had received many threats and horrible letters. It never changed his demeanor. Henry was class, but you could tell nobody wanted this to end more than him. I can't imagine the pressure, but I wish I had that swing.

April 8, 1974, Al Downing, a left-handed pitcher with the Dodgers, delivered a pitch out over the plate. Henry circled the bases, history had been made, number 715. I remember, just for a second, thinking I'm about 700 short.

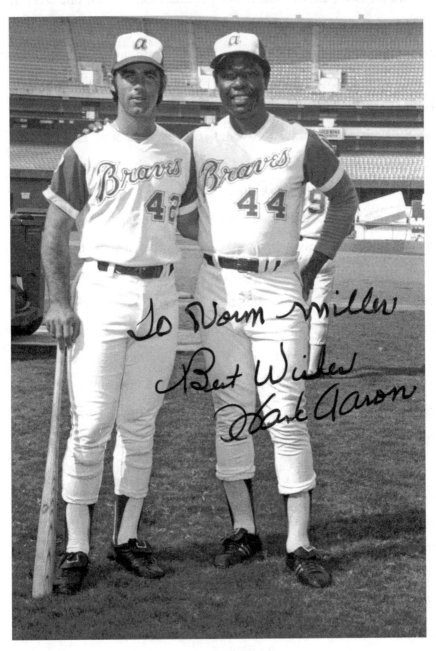

Two long-ball hitters

What a scene, what a night and there I sat in the clubhouse after the game listening to the same Hank Aaron answer the same stupid questions with class.

Things settled down and I settled into right field. Then, in the second game of the season, I dove for a fly ball and the moment I hit the ground, I knew. That's it. My back was shot.

I got up and could barely straighten up. The pain was bad. I slowly made it to the dugout and told the trainer, "That's it." As I lay on the training table, I knew I'd had enough. No more doctors. No more treatments. My spirit was broken.

Back on the disabled list, I rested at home for a few days. I sat on the couch, just watching my daughter play. The ball club called and wanted me to come in for an examination. I didn't want to go, but what choice did I have? It wasn't good. They said I needed to come in every day and get treatment and do a lot of walking. I wanted to just go back to Texas and call it a career.

Later on in the summer, I called Eddie Robinson and simply asked him to release me, I'm finished. For some reason, he wouldn't do that and I kept riding in every day and taking walks around the outfield. The worst thing was the feeling of not being part of the team.

But ballplayers will always figure out a way to have fun. With about a month to go, the Braves had found out that Frank Tepedino, a backup first baseman, had been living in the clubhouse. Not bad, if you think about it. No commute from the suburbs every day, you always had food and you could do your laundry right there. I invited Frank to come out and live with us for the remainder of the season, but it had one condition.

Davey Johnson, Gary Gentry, Danny Frisella and I had bought an old Cadillac limousine from a whorehouse in Atlanta. We told Frankie he would have to be our driver. He was good with that. We bought him a chauffeur's hat. Every day, we'd put a quart of oil in the beast and head to the ball yard. Frankie was a fine driver, but he wouldn't open our doors.

I didn't make any of the road trips, I just hung out at the apartment waiting for the season and my career to come to an end. I packed Vicki and Aly up and sent them home and I would be driving home alone.

This Guy Must Be Nuts

A few days before the season ended, Clyde King called me into his office. I took a seat in front of his desk. "Norm, you know what I'm holding here?" "No, Clyde, I don't."

"This is the opening-day lineup for next season and you're hitting fifth." I looked at Clyde like he was nuts. I told him, "You better have a long bat for me, because I'm going to be home in Sugar Land, Texas." What could he be thinking? I've played a handful of games in two years with the Braves. Hell, I hadn't put on my jock for two months. You don't need a cup to walk around the ballpark. I wasn't sure of his motivation but I was sure it wasn't necessary.

The last night of the season came. A full house came to see their hero, Hank Aaron, play his last game as an Atlanta Brave. He had announced he was going to finish his career in Milwaukee where he started when the Braves were there.

What a finale! His second time up, he hit his last home run in the National League. He circled the bases and went up the tunnel and into the clubhouse. No curtain calls, no fan fair. He was already out of his uniform when I went up to see him. He handed me his cleats and said, "Here, these are for you." He walked out, got in his Chevy and drove off. That was it. Ladies and gentlemen, Hank Aaron has left the ballpark.

I Turned On The Radio And The Fat Lady Was Singing

A couple of hours later, it was my turn. I said my good-byes, wished everybody well and walked out. I got in my Mercedes and headed out of the stadium tunnel, a couple of left turns and I was on the interstate heading home.

I glanced over at Fulton County Stadium, a terrible looking stadium by the way, and waved good-bye. See you, baseball, you're the best. I wasn't upset, sad or pissed off; I was actually relieved. I had a long drive ahead. So I just started talking to myself. About 800 miles of memories to talk about.

It seemed like one big circle since that day I drove to Anaheim for my first spring training. I remember how confident I was. Most thought I was just too small to make it. I didn't care what people thought. I knew from day one when my dad played that first game of catch with me that this was fun and what I wanted to do.

I started to think about those guys from the first year. Is Jim Sollami shooting pool tonight? Whatever happened to Jim Tokas and one of my favorites, Pete Gongola? There were so many guys that I thought would make it and yet they didn't. I kind of wondered why.

Of course, the longer you play, the more you realize just how good you have to be, and a little luck certainly helps.

Some guys never get out of the low minor leagues. There's a reason. Some get close to the big leagues, but just fall short. There's a reason. Maybe they can't hit the curve ball or they can only play one position and it never opens up. There's always a reason though, because the cream does rise to the top.

I pulled into a little store to load up on snacks; it's going to be a long night. Twinkies, Cokes, and chips, you can't beat it. Junk food, rock and roll music on the open road in the middle of the night. Something very serene to me about that.

Kind of like when the team would be flying in the middle of the night, the plane would be quiet except for the guys playing cards in the back. I would just stare out the window, looking at the moon. Every once in a while I would just glance around and see my favorite baseball players and realize, how cool is this.

Over the years, I got to sit in the cockpit on many flights. Since they were charters, it was pretty easy to do. I remember one night flying back to Houston from Montreal. It was about 3:00 AM, beautiful night. The captain got up to stretch and told me to hop in his seat. This was cool. Then he reached over and pushed a button and said, "You're flying it. Go ahead, turn the wheel a little to the right. That's it, now come back to the left." Oh my god, the feeling of control I had was amazing. Back on auto-pilot, the captain took over. I walked back into the cabin. Someone asked me, "Who's flying this thing, why the turns?" I just smiled and said, I was. He didn't believe me. That's probably a good thing.

You know, when I started to think about defining moments in my career, I couldn't help but think of Al Monchak. That first day in my first camp when he called my name out. I remember what he said, "Show or go." Scared the hell out of me. I think that really got me off to the right start.

Then, another defining moment was when the team decided Chuck Tanner would be the right manager for me. That was big. That night he dragged me in the locker room and reamed me out changed my life. In fact, in all my years, Chuck by far was the best to play for. He sure went on to have a great career managing in the bigs. Wish we could have gotten together again, maybe things would have been different.

What if I would have stayed in the Angel organization? Would they have kept me at second base? Would there have been a position in the big leagues that I could have filled as quickly as it happened as an Astro? My mind was just racing with questions. So much went by so quickly.

I pulled over for a little while. I'm anxious to get home, but in one piece. I have a family to take care of.

Thank god I listened to the advice from Bob Rodgers about learning something else to do while I was a player. I had a great job waiting for me in Houston. Getting that real estate license paid off. I played with a lot of guys that, when I asked what they would do after they were through playing, just shrugged their shoulders. "Don't know, never really thought about it." Once you're in the game, all of us are eternal optimists. You have to be. I think everyone thinks they're going to make it. They'll make good money and get a good job after playing.

I stuff that first Twinkie down my face - need some sugar to stay awake. I'm just about in Alabama now.

I was thinking about some of the greats of the game. Let's see, catching, Johnny Bench. I remember when I first saw him. He looked like a boy-man. I mean, he was a tough-looking 18-year-old. Huge hands, great power and a cannon for an arm. No need to go to the minors. He could do it all.

First base, I would have Willie McCovey or Willie Stargell on my team. Both enormous men with unbelievable power. Stargell hit one off of Dierker into the top deck at Three Rivers one night. I think Dierker even applauded that feat. As for McCovey, I hated playing against him, especially in Candlestick Park with that high sky and wind. I would play him literally against the right field fence. He would hit those towering fly balls and I would circle and circle and catch it and fall on my ass. Routine play for me. Either one of those guys would work.

One-time Astro, Joe Morgan, at second base. Best thing ever happened to Joe was to get traded away from Harry and Spec. He went to be part of the "Big Red Machine" and his game went to another level. Little guy with confidence and desire second to none. Quick bat, quick feet and made himself a good glove-man.

Mike Schmidt from the Phillies is at third. Like Bench, from day one, you knew this guy was special. Tremendous power, good arm, great range. Clutch hitter who played every day.

Shortstop had to be Maury Wills from the Dodgers. Bunt you to death, slap the ball around, and steal a base.

The outfield, boy that's easy. Three words. Clemente, Mays, Aaron. You put those three anywhere you want. Think about those guys I played against in their prime. The question was always asked, who's better? What's the difference, I ask. My favorite to watch was Clemente. He was so wild and athletic. The best arm in the game, could hit anything thrown up there and hit it with power. Ran the bases like a wild man. It always seemed like late in the game, Clemente would be at bat. He'd get a hit, walk, get on somehow. Steal second. Steal third and then score somehow. Intimidating player. Just great.

Mays, what can you say? All the tools: hit, power, speed, arm and great glove. Came to the ballpark with the enthusiasm of a kid every day. He loved being Willie Mays. "Say hey, Willie Mays." That basket catch he made. If I tried that, I would get hit in the balls.

And Henry, the man I just watched hit another one out a few hours earlier. Smooth, effortless, all the tools, which he never got credit for because he made it look so easy. Great guy, and I'm so proud I can drive down the road knowing he's a friend.

Pitching, the top two are easy: Sandy Koufax and Bob Gibson. I never got to face Koufax, but I loved to stand right there at the bat rack and listen to guys as they came back in after being up there. Koufax had two pitches. Fastball, curveball. Both about the same speed and basically un-hittable. For about five years, nobody could touch him.

The best right-hander, Bob Gibson. Intimidating as they come and with a fastball and a breaking ball that exploded. Also would knock you down in a heartbeat. In fact, on an 0-and-2 count in St. Louis one day, he nailed me in the left elbow. As I crawled to first base and the trainer was cutting away my sleeve to see the damage, Gibson strolled over from the mound and told them to get me off the field, we were holding up the game. Prick. I went 0 for 9 years against Gibson. My last time I faced him, I hit a ground ball to Maxvill at short. I was fucking thrilled.

There were two pitchers that I'm just glad I'll never have to face again. One right-hander and one left. Both threw incredibly hard and scared me. The left-hander was Bob Veale from the Pittsburgh Pirates. A 6'10", a sidearm flame thrower. The first time I stood in the box and he dropped down to sidearm my ass flew out of the batter's box. And the next time and the next time the same result. He was frightening.

I don't feel as bad admitting fear when it comes to the right-hander. Many, especially in this pitcher's early years, didn't want to go up to the plate. Now, most won't admit that, but I've seen fear in the eyes of some of the best. That right-hander is Nolan Ryan. I'm telling you, that was a fastball like no other. And he had a great curveball - just couldn't get it over the plate very often early in his career. But that fastball gave you no time to relax because if it ever came inside, and it often did, you had so little time to react, it was just frightening. His fastball just exploded. I won't miss that and I don't mind telling you that.

Those guys were the best, but there were so many guys that could really play. I mean, stand out in the crowd. Take Richie Allen, one of the strongest guys in baseball. He always wore long-sleeve shirts because he didn't want people to see his arms. What a character. I started laughing when I thought of Richie. I remember one time when we went to Philadelphia in '69 and Larry Dierker and Don Wilson struck him out, I think eight straight times in two games. When we got to the ballpark that third day, Richie was sitting in our dugout when we came out for batting practice. "Who's pitching for you guys?" "Tom Griffin," I told him.

"You go up and tell that kid I'm going to hit the farthest home run he's ever going to give up." So I told Tommy what Richie had said. It inspired Tom to reach back and throw a fastball by him. Well, Richie's a man of his word. He hit that pitch over my head in right field, over the tower on top of the scoreboard. It had to be 600 feet when it landed. Richie just walked around the bases.

Another time, I was on first base. Richie was behind me when I took my lead. Gene Mauch, the Phillies' skipper, came out of the dugout and yelled across the field to Richie to hold me on. I wondered what he was doing behind me. Richie yelled back, "He's not going anywhere." Mauch came out further and they started to argue. Finally, Mauch returned to the dugout and Richie came up to the bag. As I started to lead off, he grabbed my pants. I turned to the umpire, but he was watching the pitcher. I looked at Richie, and he was smiling from ear to ear. Next pitch, the same thing, finally the umpire saw it and called time. He walked up to the base, trying not to laugh and reminded Richie that you can't hold the runner on by grabbing his uniform. "No problem," said Richie and he moved back behind me. I stole on the next pitch and Mauch went nuts in the dugout.

God, I met so many characters in the game. The funniest, though, had to be my roomie, Doug Rader. What a ballplayer, but what a mind. Nobody ever like him in the game before. If I told some of the stories about Doug, people wouldn't believe it. I was thinking about the night he ordered room service and when the bellman brought it up, Doug made him stay in the closet until he was through eating. Another time, he and I had to fly back to Houston from New York for an Army Reserve meeting. When we finally got on the plane in Newark, everybody was asleep. The plane had come from Boston and it had to be around 2:00 AM. I sat down in the first seat in first class; Doug went somewhere behind me. As we taxied out to the runway, suddenly the look on the stewardess in the jump seat gazing down the aisle was my first clue that something was about to happen. Then came the growling noises. As I looked back, there was Doug, covered in a blanket, cruising down the aisle in coach, waking people up.

The miles kept clicking away and I just kept driving with a smile on my face. Just thinking about the "Red Rooster" was enough to almost make me go off the road. One year, he took a corner of the locker room and made it into his own luau tent. I mean, torches and all. He would just hide in there. He always said that in his previous life he was a pirate, so this made perfect sense to all of us. Oh yeah, we were in San Francisco playing an afternoon game. I was in right field. That's a shocker. Man on first and there was a base hit to right. I came up throwing and threw a bullet to third. Ron Hunt was the base runner. He had a reputation of being a real tough, hard nose player. Nobody was better at decoying than Rader. As Hunt got close to third, Doug was standing there so casual, like there was not going to be a play. He snatched my throw and slammed the tag on Hunt's head. Hunt went straight to the ground in a sitting position. Umpire yelled, "Out," and

Hunt was literally out. I mean cold. Doug liked that. He liked inflicting pain.

Doug had a mind that thought like no other. We were waiting on a bus one day to go to the airport after getting our asses kicked in Cincinnati. It was hot as hell and Art Perkins, our traveling secretary, was the only one not on the bus. Finally, we saw Art come skipping across the parking lot. Truly one of the nicest guys in the game with one of the hardest jobs in baseball. Art looked like a biology professor, slimly built, in his 50's, always sporting a bow tie. He also had one leg shorter than the other and wore those gigantic wing tip shoes with the 20,000-mile soles on them. He was really in a hurry and that leg was really flopping. As he boarded the bus, Doug told him "Art, you know, you'd be really hard to track in a snow storm." Only Rader could make these observations.

A book had come out, written by Jim Bouton, called *Ball Four*. I think it was in 1970. Bouton, a former Yankee pitcher, was traded to our club and I was rooming with him when he was writing the book. I remember the day it came out, all the controversy. We were in New York and I was half asleep. Jim was on the phone giving an interview, when suddenly there was a banging on our door. I looked at the clock, it was 7:15 AM. I didn't move. More banging. Jim asked me to get the door. So, I got up, buck naked, and asked who it was. "This is Howard Cosell, open this door."

"Yeah, I'm fucking Superman, so take a flying leap at a rolling donut." I went back to bed. Then the banging was real serious and I was pissed. I jumped up and opened the door. Holy shit, it was Howard Cosell. He pushed me aside and grabbed the phone from Jim. "This is

Howard Cosell, and this interview is over." He slammed down the phone. I did not get dressed for the bastard, I just lay there, naked.

One of the stories in Jim's book was about a hole a player drilled in the dugout. Gee, I wonder who would do such a strange thing? Yours truly, that's who.

It was during my time of not playing regularly and I had spent many nights just sitting there. I had a little fingernail file, so I started probing a little every night. Kind of like escaping from Alcatraz, wondering what would be on the other side. After many nights of discreetly digging away, I saw the light. When I looked through, I was ashamed of what I had done. Panties were in sight. I was appalled and made sure nobody else looked. But I couldn't hold them back. Bad boys we are.

The next night, just out of curiosity, I look out the top of the dugout to see who might be in that seat. A beautiful woman, but she looked very warm. So I got a hypodermic needle out of the trainer's bag and put some nice cool water in it. Stuck it through the hole in the dugout and cooled her down. Mean trick, great reaction as we peaked out of the dugout. Boredom plays havoc on my mind.

Night after night watching baseball can get to you. Tom Griffin and I would sit there like we were really into the games. One night Tom, who is really a clever guy, started to interview me. I played the role of Zino Kriskowski, Polish pitcher that had an arm transplant. That's right, I had my right arm moved behind my head so I could throw a real overhand curve ball. Well this little game ended up on an Astros pre-game show. Then one of the local radio stations wanted Tom and I to do a show. We went for a visit down at the station and managed to destroy a studio playing with the equipment. Zino Kriskowski was never heard from again.

Another night, I was asked to do the pre-game show and I announced I was retiring. I've been told it's hard to tell when I'm lying. I simply said I had enough and I wanted to go out on top. I thanked everyone in the organization and the fans and retired.

That cost me some money. Our asshole GM was listening in his box and did not think it was funny. Too bad.

Shit, I'm almost out of gas. I hope something's open at this hour.

Okay, back on the road and into Mississippi I go. Why do people live out here? Anyway, beside my first hit, I was thinking, what was the next biggest moment in my career? Let's see, maybe it was the home run I hit on my wife's birthday. Nah! How about the pinch-hit home run to beat Juan Marichal? Actually, that was pretty cool, but on the same day, Eddie Mathews hit his ... I don't know ... 512th. That was the story of the game, not my heroic pinch-hit home run. No interviews after the game. I was starving for attention. Maybe it was my grand-slam home run off the Pirates' relief ace, Elroy Face. That was good, but the score was 9 to 1, our favor, at the time. Elroy Face had the best forkball in baseball but once in a while, like once a year, he throws his 80-mile-per-hour fastball and guess who got it? Elroy kind of said, "Here, hit this." That made the score 13 to 1. What a clutch hit.

I would catch batting practice once in a while just to do something different. The ball club didn't care. They probably hoped I'd get a foul ball in the nuts. So, once in a while, depending on the ballpark we were at, rather than sit in the dugout, I would go out to the bullpen. I remember old Connie Mack Stadium in Philly, they had a door in the bullpen that led out to the street and you could go get a sandwich on the corner.

At a couple of ballparks, they would store the batting cages out in the bullpens. They folded up just right so the net would make a hammock and I could get some much-needed sleep during the game. Once, I fell asleep in the bullpen in San Francisco and the goddamn camera caught me. The boss loved that back home as he watched it on TV. Another $100 to the kitty.

One of the strangest things that happened to me was when I got called out on strikes on a pitchout. We were in the Dome against the Dodgers. Sutton was pitching, Jeff Torborg catching. Al Barlick was the umpire. He was also known as "St. Peter." Runner on first, the count two balls and two strikes with two outs. A good time to try to steal a base. The Dodgers must have been thinking that too. Sutton wound up and threw a pitchout – he threw the ball 'way outside the plate so that the catcher would be in good position to make the throw to second base to catch the runner who was trying to steal. Torborg fired to second to get the runner and Barlick yelled, "Strike 3." He called me out on a fucking pitchout. The ball was nowhere near the plate. I went beyond ballistic. I threw shit everywhere and called him everything. They had to put me in a straight jacket. The next day I was fined by the league and received a letter stating I could no longer talk to Mr. Barlick or even look at him.

The next night I was starting in left field. As I ran out to my position, Barlick yelled, "Don't look at me." What a nut bucket.

I'm getting tired, maybe I'll pull over here for a little nap. I'll be back!

Whew, I needed that. Anyway, I think the thing I'll miss the most is the lunacy of the locker room. I mean it's a strange place. We spend countless hours secluded under the stands. So much down time. Some guys just hang out in their lockers; others like to stir up shit. There's always someone on someone else. If people were allowed into that room they would think we hate each other. But it's about nine months of brotherly love. Just a little disjointed at times. I mean, naked men walking around holding onto their dicks like they might get away. People cutting the crotch out of your pants for laughs. Cherry bombs thrown in your locker. That happened one night and Jimmy Wynn almost got killed getting away from it. No harm, no foul, I guess.

I remember we got a player from the Yankees. When he arrived, they put him in the locker next to me. He could do something I never saw before. It's not like we sit around and look at each other, but when a guy has to wind his dick to get it into his jock, that's impressive. It was so big, it had its own respiratory system. I moved my locker the next day.

The weirdest dick thing I ever saw was when a player put his unit in a hot dog bun and covered it in mustard and relish and laid it on a plate. While being interviewed at his locker he suddenly stood up and his hot dog fell out of the bun, but didn't hit the floor. I don't think I ever laughed so hard in my life. This was genius. Reporters were repulsed.

I'm almost home. I'm getting a little goofy. I can't believe it's over. I'm 28 years old and I've been throwing that ball around since I was about six. I loved it. I joke a lot about my career but deep down, goddamn, what if?

The places I've been, the people I've met and the guys I played the game with, how lucky I was.

I mean, when it comes right down to it, I did it all! I hit a grand slam and I struck out with the bases loaded. I made a beautiful catch in right field and I dropped one in front of 40,000 people. I stole a base and got picked off more than once. I rode the buses and I soared in the planes. I stayed in dumps and made pocket change. I stayed in the best and drove a Mercedes. The game was good to me.

Finally I'm pulling into my driveway. I am exhausted from driving and my cheeks hurt from laughing about the things I saw and did the past 11 years. I shut the garage door on a mediocre career.

But one helluva a great time.

You Have Got To Be Kidding Me

I settled into being a full-time husband and father and started a new career. Then, in January of '75 I got a phone call that I wasn't expecting. It was Al Campanis, General Manager of the Los Angeles Dodgers.

Subject to me taking a physical, they would like to sign me as a pinch hitter. I told him I would have to think about it. This was agony. I had made up my mind it was over, my back needed surgery and I had a great job. But ...

I talked with my wife and I told her if it wasn't for it being the Dodgers I wouldn't even consider it. She said, "Who are you kidding, if it was the Tokyo Giants you'd go."

The doctor said I should be able to make through the season, as long as I was just a pinch hitter.

I called my folks and told them I was a Dodger. Dad was beside himself.

The day came to head to "Dodgertown." You talk about first class, this was it. Great living conditions, a pool, tennis courts, golf course and their own airplane, the only pro team to have one.

It's always exciting to walk into that clubhouse the first morning. There was Bill Buckner, Bill Russell, Don Sutton, Steve Garvey, Steve Yeager - all the greats that I had played against for years. I unpacked the old jock and here we go again.

Walt Alston the manager for over 20 winning years came in the room. Everything just kind of got quiet as he took a seat in the middle of the room. Walt calmly lit up a cigarette and gazed around the room.

Every spring the managers would give this opening-day bullshit speech. Excuse me, motivational talk.

Walt just smiled. "Welcome guys. I hope you and your families had a nice off season. We have added more batting cages this year, plenty of kids to pick up the balls for you. The coaches are all ready to give you as much extra work as you need. We have an extra masseuse for those tired muscles, so that's good. Enjoy the pool, take it easy on the tennis court and if you play golf make sure you walk, no carts. Opening day is just five weeks away so if you're ready you'll be hopping on the plane for LA, if not, good luck."

I've never been in a more fun baseball atmosphere and saw so many guys that worked their asses off.

I was getting a lot of chances to swing the bat, but I wasn't getting any hits.

Then the day came when I actually knew it might be over for me. I'm a high-fastball hitter, we were in the last week of spring training and I was still missing my pitch. I had lost that little edge and knew it.

Finished, Done, Stick A Fork In Me

Camp broke to head to LA. We had a couple of exhibition games against our cross-town rivals, the Angels. After the first game I was called into the skipper's office. I was told I was being released. You know, I expected it but this hurt. I knew I had to go outside and break the news to my dad.

My dad just smiled, shook my hand and told me, "Hey you did it, you made it to the big leagues. What else can ask for?" What a great guy.

When I landed in Houston, I smiled at my wife and said "If anybody calls me, just tell them I'm not home and you don't know where I am."

That was many years ago and to this day I am so thankful that I am one of the very few that gets to play major-league baseball.

The characters, the fun and knowing that I was a ballplayer is something I proudly live with everyday.

As the years pass, you realize the fans don't remember your stats (thank god), but they remember how you played. They've been great to me.

Thanks to my dad for spending so much time with me as a kid, teaching me the game.

Thanks to Chuck Tanner for dragging me into the locker room and teaching me what a professional is.

Thanks to all my teammates, you crazy bastards. And thanks to all you pitchers that threw me high fastballs. And fuck all you curve ball pitchers. I hope your arms have fallen off.

Acknowledgements

Y ou ought to write a book - I heard it so many times, so thanks to all of you that actually thought I had something to say.

Thanks to Beth Webster for her spirit and wit. To Jim Barham for his honesty, friendship and creative support. And Bill Large for his talent and his laughter.

To my wife for having to live with me for over 40 years, and my mom and dad for allowing me to love the game above everything else.

To EVN Consulting (http://www.evnconsulting.com) for getting me through all the technical and marketing hurdles it takes to do this kind of thing.

My appreciation to the following organizations for their cooperation in the publishing of this book:

Houston Astros Baseball Club

Atlanta Braves Baseball Club

Los Angeles Angels of Anaheim Baseball Club

Associated Press

A special thanks to Radkey Jolink for shooting the front and back covers.

Finally, my sincere appreciation to everyone that reads this book. Thank you and be sure to tell your friends.

About The Author

Norm Miller

I first knew I wanted to play professional baseball the moment I got my first hit in Little League. The desire only grew as I continued through high school. Then I got my chance.

I signed out of high school and went on to play professionally for 12 years. After a few years in the minor leagues I made it up with the Houston Astros. I finished my career with the Atlanta Braves in 1974.

I played with and against some of the greatest of all times. I was there when Mickey Mantle hit the first home run in the Astrodome. I was a teammate when Henry Aaron broke Babe Ruth's record.

On a personal note, I did it all. Maybe not as much as some, but from a grand slam to a walk off home run, to striking out to end the game, I missed nothing.

When it was over, my wife and I made Houston our home.

For over 30-plus years, I have had a wonderful career in marketing and advertising.

For the past 13 years I have been associated with a publicly–traded bank headquartered in Houston.

My two daughters and two granddaughters live close by, so family life is excellent.

When I'm not working on something creative for the bank, I play a little golf, travel, and just enjoy life.

After a cancer scare five years ago, I'm just glad to be here.